RE-EDUCATING THE CORPORATION

RE-EDUCATING THE CORPORATION

FOUNDATIONS FOR THE LEARNING ORGANIZATION

DANIEL R. TOBIN

omneo

AN IMPRINT OF
OLIVER WIGHT PUBLICATIONS, INC.
85 ALLEN MARTIN DRIVE
ESSEX JUNCTION, VT 05452

Oliver Wight Publications books may be purchased
for educational, business, or sales promotional use.
For information, please call or write:
Special Sales Department,
Oliver Wight Publications, Inc.,
85 Allen Martin Drive, Essex Junction, VT 05452.
Telephone: (800) 343-0625 or (802) 878-8161;
Fax: (802) 878-3384.

Library of Congress Catalog Card Number: 93-060677

ISBN: 0-939246-48-1

Printed on acid-free paper.

Manufactured in the United States of America.

1   3   5   7   9   10   8   6   4   2

For Susan and Molly

ACKNOWLEDGMENTS

There are many people to thank for providing help and encouragement as I undertook the research and writing of this book. Barbara Mroz, my former manager at Digital Equipment Corporation, encouraged me when I made the decision to leave Digital and acted as a reviewer for the manuscript. Many other friends, both current and former Digital employees, also provided ongoing support and encouragement.

Early on in my research, Mark Stratton, director of education for the Society of Manufacturing Engineers (SME), invited me to participate in a meeting of the SME President's Committee on Lifelong Learning. Not only did I find the day's meeting most interesting, I also met several people there who would provide field research sites.

Jerry Wright, manager of the Caterpillar Training Institute, was my host for several days of interviews at Caterpillar. Along with many excellent members of the Training Institute, he arranged interviews with such people as Jim Despain, vice president and general manager of the Track-Type Tractor Business Unit, and

Wayne Zimmerman, corporate vice president of human services. I especially appreciated the time these gentlemen took from their busy schedules given their current contract discord with the United Auto Workers. Jerry Wright also served as a reviewer of the manuscript.

David Hogg, manager of continuous improvement and TQM for the Giffels Group, was chairman of the SME Committee and went out of his way to help me make contacts at several Ontario companies. Dave also acted as a reviewer and provided an opportunity for me to test some of the ideas at an early stage with a group of consultants from the Giffels Group.

James Marchant, Northern Telecom Limited vice president of employee and labor relations, and Lynn Evans, director of human resources at NT's Bramalea Plant, arranged a fascinating day of interviews at that plant. While there were too many people at the Bramalea Plant to list here, I am especially appreciative of the time given to me by Marg Edwards and her team in the Circuit-Pack Area.

Ken Hammill, vice president of Blount Canada Ltd., opened the doors of their Guelph, Ontario plant and arranged for me to meet with quality manager Dan Lawson and business unit manager Eugene Kraemer to discuss both the long history of Blount programs (going back to the mid-1980s, when the company was called Omark) and their ongoing improvement efforts.

Another member of the SME committee was David Baumann of United Technologies–Carrier Corporation, who introduced me to Dan Sirmans and Ralph Bott of Carrier's Organization Development and Training Department.

At NYPRO, Paul Jensen, director of the NYPRO Training Institute, Brian Jones, president of the NYPRO Clinton Plant, and corporate CEO Gordon Lankton were all excellent sources of outstanding practices.

Dr. Steven Bomba, vice president of technology for Johnson Controls, Inc., introduced me to the concept of the "teaching factory" and arranged for me to see it in action at the Great Lakes Composites Consortium.

Steve McIntosh, director of training, development, and education at PPG Industries, took time from his busy schedule to provide me with additional information about his group to supplement his article in *Training and Development*.

Other reviewers, who provided valuable comments and suggestions along the way, included Joe Heim from the Manufacturing Studies Board of the National Research Council (now on the faculty of the University of Washington), Chuck Elliott, director of professional development for Arizona State University's College of Engineering and Applied Sciences, and Phil Trimble, executive director of SME.

I would also like to thank my agent, Mike Snell, who taught me a great deal about writing a book proposal and the publishing business, and Jim Childs, my outstanding editor at Oliver Wight Publications, who taught me how to write for a business audience.

Finally, I would like to thank my wife, Susan, who provided constant encouragement and support, and my daughter, Molly, for being Molly.

CONTENTS

CONTENTS

CHAPTER THREE. THE "THINKING" LITERACY CHALLENGE

CONTENTS

CONTENTS

LIST OF
TABLES AND FIGURES

TABLES

FIGURES

INTRODUCTION

During more than a decade working for Digital Equipment Corporation, I was immersed in the company's remarkable technologies and how they could be and were used by businesses across the globe. As part of Digital's Networks and Communications Group, I trained Digital personnel and their customers on the business benefits that could be gained by the use of networking technologies.

Over the years, I have observed many companies that had invested millions of dollars in technologies (from Digital and every other major computer vendor) to help transform their operations. These investments were made under the banners of Total Quality Management (TQM), Computer-Integrated Manufacturing (CIM), Concurrent Engineering/Integrated Product Development (CE/IPD), or Business Process Reengineering. For many of the executives, these were "bet your job," if not "bet your company," investments. Unfortunately, many companies looked back on these large investments a year or two later and asked, "Why hasn't anything changed? Where's the return on our investment?"

The answer for most of these companies is that they hadn't done anything to bring their people, their organization, and their business practices along with the technologies. What was missing was a set of solid foundations of organizational design, leadership skills, and management practice to support the superstructures of higher-level technologies and methodologies.

Since leaving Digital in 1992, I have been working as an independent consultant on corporate change programs and corporate learning strategies. My research—both for my consulting practice and this book—has focused on companies that are aspiring to become "learning organizations," or to otherwise transform themselves using TQM, Business Process Reengineering, or other similar programs.

In visiting numerous companies and reading about many others, two major premises for my work and this book have emerged.

First, companies that are seeking to transform themselves into learning organizations must establish a series of solid foundations, built around the company's most valuable asset, its people, to support the superstructures of high-level business practices, methodologies, and technologies.

Business managers tend to focus their attention on operations, technologies, and financial results. While these are all vital considerations, managers may overlook the fact that it is their *people* who run the operations, *people* who use the technologies, and *people* who both earn and spend the company's money.

In today's corporation, and even more in tomorrow's increasingly competitive global economy, *knowledge* assets will be even more important and valuable than a company's physical assets. Physical assets (plant and equipment) can be easily replicated anywhere in the world, almost overnight. Any real competitive advantage must therefore come from a company's knowledge assets— assets embodied in the company's people.

The five foundations for the learning organization together

form a solid basis for maximizing a company's knowledge assets. They enable a company's employees to learn and to apply that learning to find new and better ways of working, to develop creative products and services in response to customers' existing and emerging needs, and to maximize returns on both physical and knowledge assets. In companies where the foundations are solidly in place, there is an evident level of energy and excitement as employees at all levels go about the daily task of creating the future, both for their company and for themselves.

Building these foundations requires commitment on the part of a company's leadership. Without this commitment, change cannot happen. By mission and role, the group that I would look to for assistance in building these foundations is a company's training and development organization.

In many companies I have worked with and researched, I met with both their business leaders and their training and development group managers. I often found business leaders who would look for assistance almost anywhere but their own internal training and development groups. Internal training departments were just not seen as being able to help with major change efforts. In fact, most top business managers had little knowledge of what their training and development groups actually did in the company.

At the same time, I encountered training and development groups, residing within the company's human resources department, that gave regularly scheduled skills courses to those employees who enrolled, but that weren't in any way involved in their companies' major business initiatives.

"Why aren't you out there leading the charge toward new directions?" I asked.

"We'd really like to help", was a typical response. "But we can't even get to the decision makers to discuss what we can do. So we just sit here doing our thing, collecting our rating sheets and showing our managers how well we are doing so we can keep getting our budgets and do it all over again."

At one company, my meeting with the training and development manager was interrupted by an overseas telephone call. While he took the call, I wandered around his office looking at what he had on the walls. One item was a framed copy of the interoffice memorandum announcing his hiring into the firm. At the bottom of the memo was a handwritten note from the company president welcoming him on board.

"Why did you frame this?" I asked when he finished the call.

"Because I know that that's probably the only time in my career in this company that I will ever receive a personal communication from the company president."

It doesn't have to be that way. I believe that training and development groups can have a great impact on their companies' success. It's not always easy to get the ear of the top business leaders, but it is possible. In fact, I believe that most top business managers would be thrilled if their company's training and development manager asked to help with the company's major change initiatives and actually offered ideas about how to make change more effective. Training and development groups can align themselves with their companies' strategic business directions and can sit on the highest-level company planning committees. This leads to the second premise:

Training and development organizations must be an integral part of all corporate transformation efforts and have a key role to play in planning and implementing those efforts. But to do this, training and development organizations must start by transforming themselves.

I have been fortunate over the past two decades of working in both industry and academia to have had a number of managers who have encouraged me to break traditions, to try new approaches, and to experiment with new learning methods. Donald Donato was president of Quinsigamond Community College in Worcester, Massachusetts, when I worked there in the late 1970s.

He encouraged me to build stronger ties between the college and the community and to build new programs that would strengthen the college's contributions to local business and industry.

During my years at Digital, I received support and encouragement from managers like Tom Karpowski, Bob Murray, and Barbara Mroz to push the envelope and test new learning methods, to expand my views from Digital's traditional technology focus to the larger business and organizational issues so germane to the success of Digital and its customers. While at Digital, I also had the opportunity to work with some outstanding professors, who shared many of the views expressed in this book, and who cooperated in a number of programs with the groups I represented. Among these are Richard Chase, director of the Center for Operations Management Education and Research (COMER) at the University of Southern California Business School, Dan Shunk, director of the CIM Systems Research Center at Arizona State University, and Robert Eccles and Nitin Nohria from the Harvard Business School.

It is through all of these experiences and all of these terrific people that I have built the concept of the foundations for the learning organization. Only by erecting solid foundations and by integrating the organizational and human dimensions into all transformation efforts can companies succeed in becoming true learning organizations.

This book is intended for two primary audiences. First, business managers must realize that transforming their companies involves more than issuing orders, raising a new banner, and bringing in a few high-priced consultants. It takes commitment to building and maintaining a set of solid foundations composed of organizational design, management practice, and the capabilities of the company's most valuable asset—its people. The second audience for this book is composed of the human resources and the training and development professionals who are seeking better ways of supporting their companies' transformation efforts.

It is my hope that this book will help both audiences recognize the need for change and will provide some guideposts for planning your company's transformation efforts. Because of the breadth of topics being covered, it wasn't possible to provide detailed instructions on each topic. A resource guide, contained in appendix B, provides some pointers to finding resources for deeper exploration of many of the major topics discussed.

My hope is that by reading this book, you will develop a better understanding of the challenges facing your company and will find new and better ways of working to achieve the company's overall goals.

Daniel R. Tobin
Framingham, Massachusetts, 1993

A SPECIAL NOTE
TO SMALL BUSINESSES

Small businesses that are attempting to become learning organizations have both advantages and disadvantages with respect to their larger counterparts. The advantages are that they have not yet built the massive bureaucracies that continue to stifle many change efforts in larger companies. Many of the foundations of organizational design and business practice detailed in this book will therefore be much easier for smaller companies to institute. This book should provide some excellent guidance for your company's development as it continues to grow and prosper over the coming years.

The disadvantage that many smaller companies will experience is that they have not yet started a training and development function. Many small companies are so strapped for time, personnel, and funds that employee training and development has taken a backseat to more pressing needs. If your company is in this position, this book should provide some good ideas for how to approach the training and development of your people. There are many resources available in many communities to help you without making large investments. These include:

■ Small Business Development Centers (SBDC).

■ Local Chambers of Commerce.

■ The U.S. Small Business Administration.

■ Local community colleges, four-year colleges, and universities.

■ Manufacturing Technology Centers sponsored by the National Institute for Standards and Technology (NIST).

■ The new series of "Teaching Factories" being sponsored by the federal government through the National Center for Manufacturing Sciences.

The stories from large and medium-sized manufacturers throughout this book will provide a wide range of ideas on how small business can plan and implement effective training and development activities and themselves become learning organizations.

RE-EDUCATING
THE CORPORATION

ONE

FOUNDATIONS FOR
THE LEARNING ORGANIZATION

The knowledge your company needs to succeed today *and* tomorrow already exists within its boundaries or can be accessed readily from outside sources. But most organizations don't know how to capture this knowledge and, then, how to disseminate it effectively to those who need it most. In successful organizations, knowledge provides a key competitive advantage. No matter where it resides, it is sought out, captured, and applied to solve existing problems and to create new opportunities for the future. Within these enterprises, great ideas come from every level, location, and team. Each idea is prized for its value, rather than the corporate level of its source. And when ideas, and knowledge, are shared, problems can be solved cooperatively. For example:

> The service technician was stumped. None of the standard diagnostic procedures could locate the problem with the customer's equipment. As he described the symptoms into his microphone, he heard, through his earphone, the voice of another technician who was working at another customer's

site fifty miles away: "I ran into the same problem last week. Here's what you need to do. . . ."

The design team was trying to leapfrog the competition with its next-generation product. Everything was falling into place, except the product packaging—it would require a radically new design with which the team had no experience. They sent the basic specifications across the electronic network to their packaging vendor, located some two thousand miles away. Within forty-eight hours, the team received, again across the network, a new design. In addition, several suggestions were included relating to other elements of the product that would facilitate its manufacturing process as well as substantially reduce its cost.

In successful organizations, these solutions are not developed serendipitously, but are an integral part of the organization's culture and design. Competitive advantage comes from knowledge, and knowledge comes from learning. Employees at all levels, in all functions, from all parts of the company, are conditioned both to share ideas and to learn from each other, from any and all sources inside and outside the organization. They are part of a *learning organization*.

THE "LEARNING ORGANIZATION"

In learning organizations, ideas and solutions come from everyone in the company, no matter what their functions, job descriptions, or locations. The organization taps into the cumulative knowledge of its entire value chain, suppliers and customers included, to create value.

It is the learning organization that lays the foundation for innovation, efficiency, and competitiveness in the world economy of today and tomorrow. Whether a company uses Total Quality

Management, Business Process Reengineering, or any of the other "hot" transformation programs, if it is to succeed, the following three characteristics of the learning organization must be present:

- An openness to new ideas.

- A culture that encourages, and provides opportunities for, learning and innovation.

- Widespread knowledge of the organization's overall goals and objectives and understanding of how each person's work contributes to them.

Transformation programs are built on learning—learning new tools and methods, learning to use new technologies, learning to work together across functional, organizational, company, and national boundaries. The purpose of all this learning is to create new *knowledge*, for it is knowledge that furnishes the competitive edge, for individuals, companies, and even nations. As U.S. secretary of labor Robert B. Reich points out, "Cumulative skills and insights, upon which future innovations are based, make up the nation's key technological assets. They will be lost only if insufficiently nurtured and developed."[1]

But if new learning is to be possible, thus creating the learning organization, there must also be a willingness to change old, comfortable patterns.

LEARNING AND CHANGING

Learning and changing are closely related: organizations must learn in order to change, and must be open to change in order to learn. Consultant Beverly Goldberg describes this problem well:

Every time we turn around today, we need to learn the names of newly independent nations, deal with increasingly complex federal regulations, adapt to new technologies, do business in ways that take environmental concerns into account, and find ways to reengineer the business processes we use to decrease time-to-market and lower costs. All these events require changes in the work that people do, the way they do it, the environments they work in, the power structures that govern their organizations, the skill sets they have, and the ways in which performance rewards are handled. But change is never easy.[2]

Too few companies, large or small, are succeeding in their quest to change or to learn. They adhere to the old familiar formulas that helped them succeed in the first place: "Our methods worked to build the company, so why shouldn't they continue to work?" When trouble arises, people work harder and throw more resources at the problems, failing to diagnose what the real difficulty might be—failing to learn. They continue "business as usual," even though their circumstances may have changed. In many ways, their experiences are mirror images of those faced by the managers in the following story.

THE DEER HUNTERS

Fred, Dave, and Don were having a tough time. Although they had been successful in creating a machine tool company and expanding it during the past five years, they were now stymied. The competition consistently was beating them to market with new products, and customers were growing dissatisfied with the company's lack of innovation. Several key employees were leaving to start their own company, which would then become a new competitor. In the past year, the partners had tried Computer-Integrated Manufacturing, TQM, and Concurrent Engineering, and they had invested in new workstations and milling machines. But the situation was only getting worse.

One Friday, Don turned to his two friends and said, "We've got to get out of here for a while and clear our heads. Maybe then we'll be able to come up with a new idea that will turn this place around. What do you say we go deer hunting?"

It was decided! A hunting trip in the northern Maine wilderness would cure their managerial woes. Driving to Portland, the trio chartered a seaplane that dropped them off in the unsettled forest, eighty miles from civilization and three hundred miles from the nearest customer.

As the pilot approached a lake, their destination, he told his three passengers, "Look, before you start hunting, decide which one of you will be bringing back a deer. On the return trip, this plane will hold only you, your gear, and *one* deer."

The managers said they understood, the plane landed, the hunters unloaded their gear, and the pilot took off. When the plane returned a week later, the pilot taxied over to the shore to find the three managers waiting with their gear and *three* deer.

"Look, guys," he said angrily, "I told you when I dropped you off—the plane will only carry you, your gear, and *one* deer."

"No, you look," asserted Dave. "A couple of years ago, we were in this exact same situation. We chartered the same model of plane you are flying. The pilot told us we could bring back only one deer, and he got angry when he came back and saw that we had three. But we gave him an extra hundred dollars; and he agreed to take all three."

"Okay," said the pilot hesitatingly, "give me the hundred dollars."

The transaction was made, the gear and deer were

jammed into the available space. The pilot taxied to the very end of the lake to get the longest runway possible. The plane struggled and struggled, and finally made it off the water's surface. But the load was too much—not being able to climb fast enough, the plane didn't clear the tree line at the shore and crashed.

Fortunately, the plane wasn't high enough and its slow air speed allowed it to pinwheel down a ninety-foot pine tree. As Fred climbed out of the wreckage, holding his head in his hands, he moaned, "What happened? Where are we?"

Dave looked around and said, "I'd say we're about a hundred yards . . . from where we ended up last time."

These managers were trying to transform their company but had obvious problems with changing their own behavior. They failed to learn from experience. As Charles Garfield states the problem, "Executives who have spent years getting ahead by dominating and controlling others now have to change the very modes of thinking and behavior that made them successful."[3]

If these three managers failed to learn to change their own thinking and behavior, their success in changing the thinking and behavior of their company is very unlikely. Unfortunately, they are not alone.

FAILED TRANSFORMATIONS

Many American companies have spent the last decade trying to transform themselves by using CIM, TQM, Concurrent Engineering, or other well-publicized programs. No matter which solution they try, few succeed in transforming their organizations. Executives spend millions of dollars on consultants, educational programs, and technologies, only to look back at their efforts a year or two later and ask, "Why hasn't anything changed? Where's the return on our investment?"

National surveys of companies by consulting firms such as Arthur D. Little, Ernst & Young, McKinsey & Co., and others, have found that only between 20 and 36 percent of companies that have undertaken TQM programs have achieved either "significant" or even "tangible" improvements in quality, productivity, competitiveness, or financial return.

So why doesn't change happen? Do all these consultants and vendors sell only dreams? Are the well-publicized corporate success stories only illusions, the promised results accomplished with smoke and mirrors?

The answer is that virtually all of the hype and glitter of change programs is focused on their high-level methodologies and practices, tools and technologies. We frequently hear that:

- Statistical Process Control (SPC) will solve your quality problems!

- Our newest CAD/CAM workstations will allow your engineering and manufacturing departments to work together!

- Tie your suppliers into your electronic network and implement JIT today!

But these methodologies and tools are just superstructure, and if they are to succeed in the face of the massive resistance that accompanies all change efforts, each one must be based on solid foundations. Without solid foundations, the superstructure will bend in the wind and shake when the earth rumbles. If there is no solid base for major initiatives, the entire superstructure will eventually come crashing down or, at best, be abandoned in favor of the old, more familiar structures of past experience. This even happens to some award-winning companies, such as Florida Power & Light.

Florida Power & Light was one of the few American companies to win Japan's Deming Prize for Quality Management. And, yet, today its quality program has been all but abandoned. There are two major reasons. First, workers complained about excessive paperwork required by the program, and, second, a new CEO said he wasn't "too sure about this quality stuff." Part of this CEO's attitude can be attributed to the belief that "it tended to produce a significant number of recommendations coming up [the hierarchy], which is the opposite of [his] characteristic flow."[4]

The overall management of the company also contributed to the abandonment of the quality program. While the quality program was winning awards, the company's "diversification campaign was a disaster."[5] And at the same time as the quality program was being implemented in most parts of the company, its Turkey Point nuclear power plant, which was already on the Nuclear Regulatory Commission's "watch list," was not benefiting from the new focus on quality.[6]

Most transformation programs are based on new requirements for doing business in a world economy (see table 1.1). The shifts in basic values, needed skills, and market orientation require massive change in the ways in which everyone in the business thinks and acts.

Many of these changes can be enabled and facilitated by new technologies. Electronic networks do allow faster communications between companies and their customers and suppliers. New, networked CAD/CAM technologies do allow design engineers and manufacturing engineers to work from a common database. Statistical Process Control does give manufacturing operators more information for controlling their processes. But the tools and technologies are not enough to *cause* the actual transformations. These transformations require massive changes in organizational structure and in the roles of both individuals and teams within

Table 1.1
Conventional Business Practice vs. the Learning Organization

	Conventional Practice	**The Learning Organization**
Basic environment	■ Stable ■ Predictable ■ Local, regional, national ■ Rigid culture ■ Competition only	■ Rapid, unpredictable change ■ Unpredictable ■ Global ■ Flexible culture ■ Competition, collaboration, co-creation
Business practices	■ Based on past experience ■ Procedure-driven	■ Based on what is happening now ■ Market-driven
Business Advantage	■ Low cost based on standardization ■ Efficiency	■ Uniqueness tailored to customer needs ■ Creativity
Employee Requirements	■ Follow routine ■ Follow orders ■ Avoid risks ■ Be consistent ■ Follow procedures ■ Avoid conflict	■ Deal with exceptions ■ Solve problems, make improvements ■ Take risks ■ Be creative ■ Collaborate with others ■ Learn from conflict

those organizations. In his book, *Managing on the Edge*, Richard Tanner Pascale summarizes the problem:

> [W]hen the competitive environment pushes an organization to its limits, the old mindset no longer holds. . . . Our industrial landscape is littered not only with many failed

attempts at change, but with many partially successful and mediocre attainments.[7]

Becoming a learning organization will enable any company to successfully undertake its own transformation. Total Quality Management, Value Chain Integration, Business Process Reengineering—all of these programs depend on the learning abilities of people and organizations.

BENEFITS OF THE LEARNING ORGANIZATION

Creating a learning organization is the way to move successfully from the old world to the new, from age-old business practices to a new set of procedures that will enable your company to thrive in the coming century. The primary benefits of the learning organization, and the keys to surviving and thriving in a global competitive environment, are flexibility, responsiveness, creativity, and timeliness.

■ Flexibility
Employees learn to deal with exceptions, to solve problems that were once the bailiwick of higher levels of management, to collaborate with others, inside and outside their own functions and organizations, and to take measured risks in order to ensure the organization's success.

■ Responsiveness
New directions are based on what is happening *now* in the marketplace, not on what has happened in the past. The organization becomes *market-driven* rather than experience-driven.

■ Creativity
The company's competitive advantage becomes its ability to create unique solutions to customer needs in a timely, cost-effective fashion. Rather than getting bogged down in the tangles of the old

bureaucracy, employees in the learning organization reexamine old procedures and create more efficient and effective ways of accomplishing goals.

■ Timeliness

The learning organization recognizes that time is a key competitive advantage, that reductions in time-to-market, time-to-manufacture, time-to-ship, and all other time-based parameters are essential to compete in today's rapidly moving global marketplace. By spreading knowledge to a wider base of employees, organizations find new ways to reduce these time-related measurements.

These benefits are available to all organizations if they take the time to build the foundations and if they make the investments necessary to become a learning organization. But, as stated earlier, learning and change go hand in hand. And when an organization introduces change, it can expect resistance. According to General Electric CEO Jack Welch, "Change has no constituency. People like the status quo." He continues, "They like the way it was. When you start changing things, the good old days look better and better. You've got to be prepared for massive resistance."[8] And this resistance comes not only from the rank and file, but from the top of the organization as well.

"Of course, we encourage learning in our people," you can almost hear the executive saying. "Look at how much we spend on employee training! If we didn't value learning, why would we spend so much money on it?" Of course, the deer hunters' company probably spent a lot of money on employee training, too, but they still repeated the same mistakes again and again.

What would a learning organization look like if you were to find one? Let's examine the principles that guide the learning organization and see what common criteria they might exhibit.

FIVE PRINCIPLES
FOR THE LEARNING ORGANIZATION

There are five basic principles for the learning organization. If all five are evident in your company, you can rightfully call yourself a learning organization.

Table 1.2
Five Principles for the Learning Organization

1. Everyone is a learner.
2. People learn from each other.
3. Learning enables change.
4. Learning is continuous.
5. Learning is an investment, not an expense.

1. Everyone Is a Learner

In the learning organization, *everyone*, from top to bottom, recognizes the need to learn and does pursue learning. No one is exempt. To have a top executive say that the people who work for her need to learn, but not acknowledge her own need to learn, precludes this principle.

While learning activities include much more than formal training programs, expenditures on training are a measurable indicator of an organization's openness to learning for its employees. Unfortunately, in today's corporate world,

"... most companies don't offer ... any training at all. Just 15,000 employers—a mere 0.5 percent of the total—account for 90 percent of the $30 billion spent on training annually, according to the American Society for Training and Development (ASTD). . . . Moreover, they lavish most of their education budgets on managers and executives, short-shrifting the three-fourths of American workers who don't hold a college degree."[9]

To assess whether your organization is committed to learning, ask a sample of people from throughout the organization what they have learned recently and in what learning activities (including, but not limited to, formal training programs) they are currently involved. In a learning organization, every person in the organization should be able to provide current, concrete examples.

> Blount Canada Ltd., a manufacturer of saw chain in Guelph, Ontario, used formal study groups to learn about Just-in-Time (JIT) manufacturing. They purchased sixty copies of Shigeo Shingo's book, *Study of Toyota Production System from Industrial Engineering Viewpoint*, and formed study teams from all levels of the organization to analyze the book and make recommendations for improving their operations.
>
> Blount's learning methods led to great increases in profitability by enabling the workers to implement a Just-in-Time (JIT) manufacturing system. Starting in the mid-1980s, they continue working their processes today, achieving an 8 to 10 percent annual increase in productivity.

2. People Learn from Each Other

In the learning organization, learning is not limited to structured education and training programs. People learn from each other, from instructors in formal programs, from listening to others in committee meetings, from informal observation of others' work practices, and in many other ways. The learning organization fosters such education by providing both formal and informal opportunities. Learning is synergistic—the total effect of learning and knowledge in the learning organization is greater than the sum of the learning and knowledge of the individuals in the organization.

What opportunities for learning are provided in your organization? Does your company provide both formal and informal opportunities outside of standard education and training programs? Are there development plans in place for every employee? Are these opportunities real?

> Coopers and Lybrand, one of the "Big Six" accounting firms, uses a groupware product called Lotus Notes to enable co-workers to organize and share financial and tax knowledge. The knowledge database also includes information from outside sources, such as Internal Revenue Service and tax court rulings. The system, which will be used by as many as two thousand auditors within the next year, "leverages a small number of very highly specialized people," according to Ellen Knapp, Coopers's vice chairwoman of technology.

3. Learning Enables Change

This principle is evident in two ways. First, openness to learning helps people recognize the need for change. As people learn, they discover that there are often better ways of doing their jobs, as well as improved methods that can help enhance their individual and organizational productivity. This personal discovery makes it much easier to accept change than if all changes are forcibly imposed by management. The achievement of this principle becomes evident when ideas for change come from the bottom up, as well as from the top down.

Second, if the organization recognizes that change and learning are closely related, it will also recognize the need to include education as part of any change effort. Change is enabled and facilitated through the education of the people who must effect any change program. Understanding why change is necessary makes it much easier for people to accept change. If this is happening in your organization, learning activities will be an integral part of all major program plans.

> At the Cadillac Motor Division, planning for training and development starts with the corporate planning committee. Training and development plans are included in the initial discussions of all major new programs, right along with plans for plant and equipment. No major change program can be initiated without an examination of its effects on employees, and without planning for the training and development needed by employees to make the change successful.

4. Learning Is Continuous

Just as "continuous improvement" is a hallmark of the Total Quality movement, so continuous (or lifelong) learning is a hallmark of the learning organization.

The President's Committee on Lifelong Learning of the Society of Manufacturing Engineers (SME) states this principle in this way:

> Lifelong learning is required for manufacturing practitioners and companies to competitively survive in the global marketplace and attain world-class stature. For the [individual], it is the process of identifying . . . and acquiring the skills and knowledge to remain competent. For the company, it is a process of developing and supporting a learning environment for all their employees.[10]

Learning must be continuous. It is not enough for an organization to say that "every employee receives forty hours of training each year." Structured and unstructured opportunities for learning must be part of each employee's daily work.

A study at Xerox showed that much of the knowledge needed to fix tough problems was shared "around the coffeepot" in the form of "war stories." This informal learning was actually being discouraged under the company's Quality Improvement program, which tried to focus people on finding new solutions, rather than rehashing old problems. According to Xerox's John Seely Brown, "By failing to recognize the value of such stories, the company was actually undermining an important part of the technicians' ability to do their job." This sharing "around the coffeepot" was, in fact, an important, though informal learning method for technicians. Eventually, Xerox equipped technicians with two-way radios so that they could continuously share problems and solutions, even while out at customer sites. In essence, they created a "virtual coffeepot."

Both formal and informal methods of learning are an integral part of "continuous learning." Study groups, quality circles, mentor meetings, computer-based conferencing, and many other methods can be used to foster an atmosphere of continuous learning. Learning opportunities occur every day as part of the normal day's business. The key is to encourage and facilitate openness to new ideas and the sharing of ideas and information.

5. Learning Is an Investment, Not an Expense

Learning organizations view educational activities as an investment in the company's future, not as an expense to be avoided. Just as expenditures on plant and equipment are classified as long-term, capital investments (rather than current expenses), so are expenditures on learning activities viewed as investments in *human* capital.

Just as the company's physical assets must be maintained, so does its stock of knowledge.

In your organization, when a learning solution is suggested, is it viewed as an investment in the future or as an expense to be avoided? When the budget reins need to be tightened, is training among the first items to be cut?

Several years ago, I attended a pilot seminar on Concurrent Engineering Methodologies, to provide a critique of the content and some coaching for the presenters. Because this was a pilot offering, the participants, a group of senior engineering and manufacturing managers from a variety of manufacturing industries, were not charged tuition. Toward the end of the final day of the seminar, I chatted with one of the attendees, an engineering vice president from a billion-dollar electrical equipment firm.

"How's it going? What do you think of the seminar?" I asked.

"It's really been terrific," he replied. "I've already learned a lot that I can turn around and put into action. It should really help the productivity of my engineering organization."

"That's great to hear," I said. "You know, this seminar is going to be offered on a regular basis at a cost of nine hundred and ninety-five dollars per participant. Is there anyone else in your company who could benefit from attending?"

"I can think of three of my direct reports who could really use this," he said. Then he stopped, stroked his chin a couple of times, and added, "But three thousand dollars is a *lot* of money to spend on *education*" [emphasis his].

This manager's reaction to spending money on education is not unusual. Education and training are "soft" expenditures. Even while he recognized the value of his attending the seminar (for free), he was having a hard time contemplating spending $3,000 to send three of his own employees to get the same training. He would rather spend the money on something more tangible. If I asked this same manager what it would cost to equip a new staff member's office, he probably would have said something like: "Well, we need to fit the office out well for someone who's on my staff. Standard issue management desk, credenza, files, table and chairs. And, of course, the latest workstation—we need that power. Probably on the order of forty to fifty thousand dollars."

Yes, but three thousand dollars is a *lot* of money to spend on *education*." What this manager didn't recognize is that the "power" is not in the workstation, but in the knowledge and ability of the employee who uses the workstation.

These five principles for the learning organization are applicable equally to Total Quality Management, Business Process Reengineering, and other transformation initiatives—all require adherence to the same principles as the learning organization, although methods, tools, and technologies for these various programs might differ.

Too few companies exist today in which all five principles are regularly in practice—the inertia of old methods is just too great. But that doesn't mean it can't be done. It all starts with building a set of foundations from which you can launch your transformation effort.

FOUNDATIONS FOR
THE LEARNING ORGANIZATION

To undertake any major transformation program, organizations must build a set of strong foundations of organizational practices and individual skills to support organizational learning. These foundations form the base upon which the superstructure of higher-level methodologies, technologies, and business practices can be erected. With these foundations in place, the learning organization and other transformation programs will be well within reach. Without these foundations, any or all of these programs is doomed to failure or, at best, will enjoy very limited success.

Analog Devices CEO Ray Stata says that:

> For me, organizational learning is a helpful concept to think about how to bring about organizational change. By organizational learning, I mean not only the acquisition of new knowledge, but the transformation of this knowledge into new skills which are manifest in behavior and action. . . . In fact, I believe the rate at which an organization learns is its only sustainable advantage.[11]

There are five foundations for the learning organization (see table 1.3). Each of the five foundations is discussed in its own chapter (chapters 2 through 6). Briefly, they are:

■ Visible Leadership
Without strong, visible leadership, from the top down and throughout the organization, no true transformation effort can fully succeed.

■ "Thinking" Literacy
The standard definition of "functional" literacy is much too narrow for the twenty-first century corporation. Not only do employees need higher levels of achievement in the "three Rs," they must also master a broad range of basic technical and nontechnical skills. This full range of skills moves them from "functional" literacy to "thinking" literacy.

■ Overcoming Functional Myopia
To achieve the learning organization, employees at all levels and in all functions within the corporation must remove their functional blinders and constantly keep in sight the larger goals and objectives of the corporation.

■ **Building and Sustaining Effective "Learning" Teams**

The purpose of teamwork is to enable individual team members to learn from each other. Effective teamwork is a requirement for all of the "hot" transformation programs. But working as part of a team goes against the way most Americans are raised and trained. Creating "learning" teams requires much more than throwing a group of people into a room and telling them to work together.

■ **Managers as Enablers**

There is an overwhelming trend in American industry to strip out levels of middle management. While it is true that industry does not need as many levels of management as it once did, middle managers are valuable resources that should not be tossed aside casually. There are new, important roles for many of these middle managers to play in helping their companies to achieve the results they seek.

RE-EDUCATING THE CORPORATION

To become a learning organization requires building strong foundations and re-educating the entire corporation, from the boardroom to the factory floor. Everyone in the company must learn to challenge the status quo, and to be constantly on the lookout for new ways of improving their own and the company's performance. No one is exempt from learning or acting.

KEY POINTS

The knowledge to succeed today and prosper in the future already exists within most companies—or is readily available. But this vital knowledge is often spread too thin, or isn't located where the problems exist, or is blocked by bureaucratic channels. In the learning organization, knowledge is shared and distributed in order to take full advantage of the cumulative knowledge of all employees.

Table 1.3
Foundations for the Learning Organization

Visible leadership
"Thinking" literacy
Overcoming functional myopia
"Learning" teams
Managers as enablers

The principles of the learning organization are equally applicable to most of today's "hot" transformation programs—Total Quality Management and Business Process Reengineering, for example—and building a learning organization can help ensure these programs' success. Without establishing a learning environment, most of these programs are doomed. Building the learning organization will help any organization to become more flexible, responsive, and creative, and will make the workings of the entire organization increasingly efficient and forward-looking.

The five principles of the learning organization are not present in most companies today. To get there from here requires building strong foundations upon which the superstructure of high-level methodologies and technologies can easily rest. The first of these foundations is strong, *visible leadership*.

TWO

LEADING THE REVOLUTION WITH VISIBLE LEADERSHIP

The regional sales vice president was dressing down the district sales manager for not following the new guidelines for sales expenses. After receiving a lengthy lecture on the new guidelines, the district manager responded, "You're sitting here telling me that we need to cut expenses. We're at a very expensive restaurant, at your insistence. As usual, you are having me pay the bill, which I will put on my expense account that you will okay. *Your actions are speaking so loudly that I can't hear a word you're saying.*"

Leadership requires more than just issuing memos announcing or supporting new programs and procedures. Leaders cannot have one set of standards for their employees and another for themselves—their own behavior must set a standard for their employees.

I'm sure that during your career you have encountered many kinds of leaders—a few who were very effective and inspiring and others who were not. A true leader is a person whom most of us seek—someone who can inspire us to excel in our own work and who gives us a "higher purpose" to strive toward.

SOURCES OF LEADERSHIP

The type of transformation effort implied by the learning organization arises from one of two causes: vision or crisis. Visionary leadership looks to the future, imagines what the organization can become, and transmits that vision throughout the organization, rallying the troops toward that vision. Crisis leadership also looks to the future, but sees a much bleaker picture. This rallying cry echoes the need to survive: "If we don't change, we won't be here."

Leaders exist at all levels of the organization, from the shop floor to the boardroom. Some leaders are recognized by their job titles and positions, while others have become informal leaders—people to whom others look for leadership. In examining leadership development practices, both groups must be included.

In the early 1980s, Ken Hammill, a manufacturing manager with Blount Canada Ltd., traveled to Japan and saw how JIT was being used in a number of factories. He returned to Blount, in Guelph, Ontario, with a lot of information, ideas, and enthusiasm for implementing JIT in his factory. Management listened to his ideas and told him plainly that they thought the promised results were impossible—they would not support him. As we learn from Richard J. Schonberger's book, *World Class Manufacturing*,[1] Hammill went ahead on his own. He bought copies of *Study of Toyota Production System from Industrial Engineering Viewpoint* by Shigeo Shingo for all shop floor workers, organized study groups, and implemented JIT practices, activities that eventually resulted in annual productivity increases of 8 to 10 percent over the past decade. Leadership, in this case, came not from the top of the house, but from the plant itself.

Whether trying to implement the learning organization, TQM, Business Process Reengineering, or other transformation initiatives—or starting from vision or crisis—effective, visible leadership is a prerequisite, the first foundation of the learning organization. To lead the revolution effectively, leaders must master a set of seven key practices (see Table 2.1).

VISION

Leading a company's transformation effort must start with a vision of the future toward which everyone in the company can work. This vision must be clear, so that it is easily understood, and bold enough to inspire employees at all levels. There must be a plan outlining the necessary steps to realize that vision—without clear-cut goals, employees may well be confused and dispirited, rather than energized.

General Electric CEO Jack Welch clearly articulated the importance to leadership of a business vision back in 1981:

> You can express a vision to a broad number of people. People have to want to buy into your vision. You can implement it and together you can all win and reward yourselves and the company. That's what a good leader does. He or she creates an open, caring relationship with every employee. If you can't articulate your business vision, if you can't get people to buy in, forget it. You won't be successful. It won't come from power and title.[2]

COMMITMENT

Many transformation initiatives fail because the organization's leaders are not committed to the program. This lack of commitment quickly becomes apparent, and members of the organization,

Table 2.1
Seven Key Leadership Practices

Vision
Commitment
Constancy
Coherence
Comprehensiveness
Confidence
Communications

no matter how much they may believe in the program personally, reach the same conclusion: "Why bother?" Commitment must be made by all leaders at all levels or the effort isn't worth undertaking at all.

> Professor Shingo from Japan addressed a group of company presidents at a quality forum at MIT.
>
> "Why," asked one chief executive, "isn't quality really taking hold in my company?"
>
> Shingo asked what the president's personal involvement had been in his company's quality efforts.
>
> "Well, I've made some speeches and I've signed requisitions for training and personnel. I've even appointed a vice president of quality."
>
> "What you have not done," replied Shingo, "is to make a personal commitment to quality." Without this personal commitment, Shingo went on to say, little progress would be made.

Commitment also means "staying the course." Becoming a learning organization is not a short-term investment, but rather entails changing the entire culture and ethic of the organization. This type of change takes time. Experts in organizational behavior estimate that without a concerted, sustained effort, total cultural change in an organization can take as long as ten years. Even with great effort, it can take from three to five years. This does not mean that positive results from these programs cannot be achieved in less time, but it *does* mean that without the commitment of the organization's leaders, any change takes much longer.

In 1990, Caterpillar changed its organizational form from a functional organization to a set of business units. Jim Despain, vice president and general manager of the Track-Type Tractor Business Unit and his department heads, are carrying the move even further. Despain and his team have established several profit and loss centers within their business unit. Each P&L unit is headed by its own team that must make its own decisions. Each team's job is to identify the obstacles to their ROA goals and to create objectives to overcome those obstacles. Despain's administrative group—the business unit leaders—describe their job as having four parts: "We set goals, then get out of the way. We cheerlead the improvement efforts and then recognize significant achievements." Jim Despain says that the hardest part of this new leadership role, as compared with the old management role in the functional organization, is "letting people come up with their own solutions, and letting them try their solutions, even if we don't like them. Sometimes it's hard because we know that the recommended solution won't work. Other times, we're pleasantly surprised when they make something work that we 'knew' couldn't solve the problem."

Despain and his team are committed to making the transformation work. They know that the people below them have to learn by trial and error, so they allow them to make their own mistakes.

CONSTANCY

Constancy is a partner to commitment. Too often, organizational politics result in one division or group asking the organization's leaders for an exemption from a new program or approach: "We're doing fine on our own. This new learning organization sure seems interesting, but it's going to divert our attention from the important work we are doing right now. Just let us go down our own path and we'll do fine."

There may be nothing wrong with this group's approach, but granting exemptions from new organizational directions is not wise. The resulting multiplicity of approaches will create political rivalries and rancor that easily can sink even the best-planned, most well-intentioned efforts. As soon as one group is granted an exemption, other groups will question why they have to follow the leader's directions, and soon there will be so many different directions being followed that all momentum will be lost. This is reportedly why General Motors took so long to really focus on quality— each division and plant was going in its own direction, each making some progress, but each unable to work with other groups that had adopted similar, but incompatible programs.

If any new program is to be successful in transforming the organization, it must span all parts of the company. Otherwise, the desired organization-wide transformation will never happen. This requires constancy by the organization's leaders.

Change takes time. People need to unlearn old ways of doing things and learn the new ways. There is a natural tendency to revert to old ways unless there is a constant reminder that the new methods are to be used. Such constancy and reinforcement are partners to commitment.

An industrial manufacturer, known for producing quality products, began its quality programs in the early 1980s. Are they as far along with the quality program as they think they should be? According to a senior line manager: "No. We could have been mining gold with our quality program. But just when we were approaching that level, the next corporate initiative program started and diverted attention from quality. So we're mining copper instead of gold. Copper is a valuable commodity, and we do produce products that are recognized as being high quality. But we dropped the ball too soon to get to the gold."

COHERENCE

The organization's leaders must ensure that all parts of the planned transformation are coherent, that all elements in the overall game plan are working toward the same goal. This is the whole thrust behind the concept of Business Process Reengineering. Often, as organizations grow, each functional group develops its own policies and procedures to ensure success according to its own metrics. This strict focus on local metrics can easily suboptimize the goals of the larger organization of which they are a part.

Several years ago, the trade press reported that Lotus Development's announcement of the latest version of its 1-2-3 product for the Apple Macintosh would be delayed six to nine months beyond its expected release date. According to the report, the team developing the new version of the product had done almost everything right—they had worked well together, met all of the feature and performance objectives for the project, and had kept to their original, ambitious development schedule. The problem arose several weeks before the expected release date when corporate officers finally were shown the product: it didn't *look* like the versions of the spreadsheet that worked on other platforms. Since Lotus was, at that time, engaged in a number of lawsuits against other companies for copying the "look" of its spreadsheets, corporate officers made a tough decision—to send the team back to make this version look like the other versions.

Organizational leaders must ensure that all policies, procedures, and objectives throughout the organization are coherent, i.e., that they relate to each other in a logical, orderly, and consistent fashion, and that they support the planned transformation. Unless all policies and practices are supportive of the new directions, confusion will reign, and people will quickly revert to their old ways of doing things.

A mail order retailer decided to emphasize company responsiveness to customers and invested a large amount of time and resources to train its telephone operators to be friendlier and more service-oriented when answering customer calls. The training was received with great enthusiasm by the target audience. Almost immediately, the company started receiving letters from customers noting how much more they enjoyed their interactions with the operators.

The program fell apart a month later when supervisors started giving operators poor evaluations for not completing calls within the organization's standard of two minutes. While the operators enjoyed their new roles with customers, and felt that they were really helping the company to improve customer relations, they were not willing to sacrifice their performance reviews and salary increases.

Even when the overall goals of the organization are clear, there is a requirement that the overall program be *consistent* (one component of coherence). For example, organizational leadership may decide to adopt quality or TQM as the overall directing principle for the desired organizational transformation. There are many approaches to instituting a TQM program, three well-known approaches being those associated with W. Edwards Deming, J. M. Juran, and Philip B. Crosby. These consultants have well-defined approaches, sets of tools and methods, and arrays of educational programs and consulting services to help organizations implement TQM. Each has a set of case studies and success stories that show how they have helped many organizations succeed in the quality revolution.

While the goals of these three approaches, and the results being strived for, are in most ways similar, they all use different methods, different philosophies, and, in some cases, different vocabularies. If some parts of the organization follow the Deming approach, others Crosby, and still others Juran, achievement of overall quality goals is very unlikely. More likely, a lot of time will be wasted in internal arguments about which approach is the "right" one, as well as misunderstandings over differing definitions for the same terms.

> A senior engineer from an industrial conglomerate told me, "We received a booklet and a videotape from the corporate CEO telling us that we were going to adopt Deming's fourteen points as the new way of doing business. A week later, we received a memo from our division president saying that we were going to do TQM our own way, using the Crosby approach. Yesterday, my group manager said we were going to start using Concurrent Engineering, that CE would be a better solution to our group's problems than TQM. So what am I supposed to be doing? Should I waste my time attending the Deming classes being sponsored by corporate, the Crosby classes being given by the division, or the CE training being given by my group? I wish all these people would make up their minds so that we can get on with our work!"

In this case, there was no real leadership at any level of the organization. There was no vision of the future and no immediate crisis. There was no coherence. The point is not to advocate any particular approach to TQM, but to emphasize that before starting a quality journey, the organization must select *one approach* and must implement it consistently and coherently across the entire company.

COMPREHENSIVENESS

To create a learning organization, leaders must ensure that the planned solutions are comprehensive. These transformations are very complex, requiring the change, elimination, restructuring, or modification of many interrelated methods, tools, processes, and procedures throughout the organization. Focusing only on some of the elements, without examination of the rest, which supply or depend on those being targeted for change, can only result in, at best, less-than-desired results or, at worst, a complete failure of the transformation program.

> In the early 1980s, Digital Equipment Corporation decided to reorganize, moving from a product-line structure to one that they felt would better respond to customer needs. In the previous structure, many product lines ran their own businesses, with dedicated sales forces, price lists, ordering systems, etc. The transition team planned most parts of the restructuring very well, but completely missed one key item—the product lines had as many as a dozen different order entry systems, none of which were compatible with the others. The company found itself essentially unable to take customer orders—resulting in lost sales, lost orders, and general chaos.

Besides oversight, there are two primary barriers to instituting comprehensive solutions in an established organization: the Not-Invented-Here (NIH) Syndrome, and the misuse of pilot programs.

The NIH Syndrome

One problem in trying to make a transformation effort comprehensive, affecting the entire company, is the NIH, or Not-Invented-Here, Syndrome. Typically, it occurs when managers refuse to accept ideas from outside their own organization: "If I admit that my colleague has a better idea than I have, that he is a better manager or leader, then I am admitting my own failure to manage and lead my group."

> A manager, whose group had just developed a new, industry-leading product in half the normal time for her company, was interviewed. She described how she had implemented a Concurrent Engineering approach in order to accomplish this ambitious goal. When she had finished her story, she was asked two questions. First, had the experience with Concurrent Engineering changed the way her group would work in the future—had they learned from experience? "Absolutely," she said. "This is the way my group is going to work from now on. And if you think these results are good, wait until you see the next product! We're already way up the learning curve."
>
> The second question was: "Given your excellent results, have you brought them to your group vice president? It sounds like the approach should be more comprehensive— that other parts of his organization could benefit from adopting your methods." Her response: "Do you think I'm CRAZY?!?"

There were three possible reasons for her last comment. First, in adopting the Concurrent Engineering approach to product development, this manager had set up some organizational practices that were not in line with company policies and procedures. For example, she had instituted group (rather than individual) measurements and rewards. As a result, she might have been concerned that her methods could get her into administrative hot water.

A second reason might have been that, given her group's outstanding results, she may have felt that they now had a competitive edge over other groups in her division when it came to allocation of resources and rewards. She might not have wanted to yield this competitive advantage.

The third possible reason, which is the one she gave, was: "Do you know what would happen if I reported the results at my vice president's staff meeting and suggested that the other groups in the division adopt Concurrent Engineering as we had? I might have gotten some dirty looks. And I certainly would have gotten some token pats on the back. But most likely everyone in the room would have said things like: 'We're really happy that you got such great results from your experiment. But you have to realize that our groups are different, and we do things our own way.' "

The NIH Syndrome is rampant in many companies today. It can only be cured by strong leadership.

Pilot Programs

In many organizations, leaders, not convinced or committed to the transformation, will stall progress by suggesting a *pilot* program. There are two types of pilot programs—one is a test of whether the program is the right one for the organization. "We'll try doing Concurrent Engineering on this next product, evaluate the results, and then decide if it is the right approach for the company." The other type of pilot program tests the best methods for implementing the program: "We are going to do TQM. We'll start with customer services to test our approach to introducing the concept, determine what training will be needed, and decide what other changes in policies and procedures we'll need to make to support it, etc. Once we are comfortable with our approach, then we'll broaden it to the rest of the company."

Former Xerox vice president and consultant Barry Bebb argues that using pilot programs to decide whether to adopt an approach is a sham. "Benchmarking with other companies should convince you of what approach to take. You then have to make a commitment. Only then might a pilot be considered as a first step toward full implementation." Taking a less-than-comprehensive approach will only perpetuate the status quo. If you are already several years behind your competition, or even if you are currently on a par with others in your industry, you can't afford to waste several years doing a pilot—you have to make a decision, and that decision must encompass *all* parts of your company.

CONFIDENCE

Just as company leaders must be comfortable with their decision to move the organization in a new direction, so they must constantly display confidence that the chosen direction is the right one. Severe changes are inevitable when a company tries to become a learning organization, and they often cause discomfort at all levels. But a confident leader who can rally the troops, reassuring them that all of the pain associated with the planned changes will in the end be worth the effort, can be very effective in keeping the revolution moving forward. Warren Bennis states it this way: "Leaders have an overall perception that their goals can be met. No matter how daunting the tasks facing leaders are, they approach them as if they can be solved."[3]

It is rare that any major transformation effort goes perfectly smoothly, with the expected benefits appearing immediately. In fact, as people start along the learning curve, progress will be very slow. Leaders who are confident of success and continually push their organizations along the learning curve will, in the end, find the length of the journey shorter than planned, and certainly shorter than if they were to allow people to jump off the learning curve periodically to ameliorate employees' complaints about the toughness of the journey.

According to Brian Jones, president of the NYPRO Clinton, Massachusetts, plant, the constant expression of confidence in the future, of the eventual success of business initiatives, is vital. "The company's focus on its quality initiative has resulted in great improvements, not only in company performance, but in employee pride and morale. We have created a culture in which people want to contribute." He points proudly to a just-completed application for the Baldrige Award. "I didn't tell them to do this. Fifty operations people spent three months working on this application." The Baldrige Award application reflects his own confidence in the success of the plant's quality efforts and shows how that confidence has been spread throughout all levels of the operation.

COMMUNICATIONS

Visible leadership requires open, clear, forthright communications. Sometimes this is called *"cheerleading."* Cheerleading is certainly part of communications—leading the charge, publicly acknowledging victories along the way, reinforcing correct behaviors. But communications involves more than just cheerleading. It also involves acknowledgment of the hard work that will be required to achieve the transformation. Employees must be assured that they will not be punished for trying and not succeeding. They also need to know that they are not alone—that the organization's leaders are struggling with many of the same issues of learning new ways and unlearning old, dealing with changes, and taking risks.

Internal Communications

Most people are willing to try new directions, such as the learning organization, if they believe that the new direction is not just the "program of the week," that there is leadership committed to helping them change, and that they will be assisted in making their personal journey. If the organization's leaders only make a speech or, worse, issue a memo endorsing the new direction and are never heard from again on the subject, uncertainty will follow.

When introducing the learning organization, what is the best method to ensure that leadership is taken seriously? Clearly, leaders who take the time to teach the new methods to their employees will be taken very seriously. NYPRO CEO Gordon Lankton puts it this way: "The most important thing you can do for an employee is to give him an opportunity to learn."

The "waterfall" approach to training, acknowledged as having started at Xerox, has each level in the organization trained by their management. If the CEO takes the time to teach the new methodologies to his or her direct reports, and they, in turn, teach it to their staffs, the message is clear throughout the organization that this is serious business—not a flash in the pan that will be replaced by another fad program next week. NYPRO Clinton president Brian Jones measures his managers on how much training they personally do for their people. Managers in his plant are the ones who organize, train, and coach teams. He says that having the managers do the training makes it clear to employees that the subject matter is important.

External Communications

Trying to implement the learning organization, or any other transformation initiative, is very likely to temporarily disrupt "business as usual." Such disruptions, however minor or temporary, surely will be noticed by the organization's external audiences, its suppliers and customers, investors and industry analysts. When starting a major initiative, the organization's leaders need to communicate with these audiences, to explain what is happening and why, and to assure them that things will soon return to normal— or even be improved. As with the organization's employees, open communications with external audiences will typically foster both understanding and enthusiastic interest.

> During a daylong session entitled "Change Management and Concurrent Engineering" given for the CIM steering committee of an aerospace corporation, the company's vice president of operations complained about a recent partnership with a computer manufacturer and a software developer to create the next generation of CAD/CAM tools. "We can't find out what's happening! They're treating us like a customer, not a partner!"
>
> If you are having trouble with developing a new product that a *customer* is relying on, you might try to hide the problem from the customer, at the same time doubling your efforts to solve the problem and giving the customer assurances that the product will be produced on time. However, as a *partner*, he went on to say, "they have a responsibility to tell us about any problems, and to ask us to help solve those problems."

LEARNING TO LEAD

Leadership practices are not intuitive. Leaders aren't born—they need to be developed. In a 1990 speech to a symposium for the MIT Leaders for Manufacturing Program, Analog Devices CEO Ray Stata publicly stated his own *mea culpa*.

> A revolutionary change of management practice and culture will not occur without very strong leadership and know-how from the top. To a large extent I have been a cheerleader and spectator of the process, but not a participant. I have not learned new skills that have materially modified my behavior and actions. Obviously that has been a foul-up in the process which can only be corrected if I

spend the same time and effort to learn as I expect from others."[4]

So how do organizational leaders learn to lead the transformation to a learning organization? How do leaders become effective revolutionaries? Leadership development requires the use of a variety of learning methods, along with coaching, reinforcement, and opportunities to practice newly acquired skills.

TODAY'S LEADERSHIP PROGRAMS

There are literally hundreds of leadership training programs available today from universities, consultants, and training vendors, along with hundreds or thousands more developed in-house by corporate training and development groups. Leadership training programs have been around, in many different forms, for more than two decades. So how come we don't have more real leaders?

McGill University professor Jay Conger studied five well-known, publicly offered leadership programs.[5] He classifies the programs according to four basic approaches to leadership development:

- Through personal growth.

- Through conceptual understanding.

- Through feedback.

- Through skill building.

The *personal growth* approach originated in the humanistic psychologies of the 1960s and 1970s. This approach assumes that in every individual there is a reservoir of personal dreams and talents that, if released, will help transform the individual into a leader. This type of program focuses on physical and psychological challenges for the individual, to help develop the self-confidence to follow those dreams and use those talents. Typical of this approach are such programs as Outward Bound and the well-known "ropes course."

The *conceptual understanding* approach helps the individual to understand what it takes to be a leader. As Harvard Business School professor John Kotter states: "The value of [this approach to] leadership training is in helping people to understand what leadership really is. This awareness building can also stimulate participants' enthusiasm about the idea of leading."[6]

Feedback approaches assume that the subject already possesses and uses some leadership skills. By providing feedback from the people who work with and for him, the individual realizes what strengths he already has and learns where he needs further development.

Finally, *skill building* approaches provide instruction and practice in specific leadership skills, which include creating and communicating a vision for the organization, getting buy-in, and inspiring employees. Skill building is the oldest of the approaches to leadership training.

While all of these approaches have some merit, no one method is really up to the task of developing leaders. The development of leaders needs to include *all of* these approaches, plus a lot more.

WHY TODAY'S LEADERSHIP
PROGRAMS DON'T TEACH PEOPLE TO LEAD

There are three primary reasons why today's leadership programs don't teach people to lead:

- Limited time span.

- External focus.

- Limitation of methods.

Limited Time Spans

Most public leadership programs run from three days to a week in length. They are one-shot, intensive efforts—you come, get your instruction or experience, and leave. There is little or no follow-up, no ongoing coaching, no reinforcement of the skills learned or attitudes acquired. A manager leaves the office on a Friday, travels to a remote location, gets her dose of leadership, and returns to the office a week later. She may have learned and changed during that week, but her job and her organization have not.

Another problem with the one-shot leadership solution is that it is likely to be crammed full of so much material that the participants cannot possibly absorb it all, let alone put it all into practice upon returning to the office. The well-known Myers-Briggs classifications, for example, present you with sixteen possible classifications, with a well-researched narrative profiling each one. These classifications used in many leadership and management development programs, provide too much information for a person to absorb in a short period of time. Most people coming out of a Myers-Briggs training session will remember their own four-letter combination and some information about what it means. They will know something about the components of the other fifteen combinations, and may even remember the combinations for one or two other people in their group. By the time they return to the office, they probably will not remember much else besides their own combinations, especially if Myers-Briggs is one of many exercises undertaken during the week.

One week of training, no matter how good, does not a leader make.

External Focus

Many of the publicly available leadership programs are individual-focused. That is, individuals from many different companies and industries sign up on a space-available basis.[7] Because of the diversity of backgrounds of the participants, the programs cannot be tailored to any one person's specific needs or organizational context. While it is certainly beneficial to share experiences with employees from different industries and different companies, the material in the course must remain generic.

The external focus also means that there will be no reinforcement once the manager returns to the office. People may ask about her experience, but otherwise it is business as usual. If she tries out some of the techniques she has learned during the week, she will get some odd stares and some comments, like "Oh! that must be something you learned in that leadership course!" But with no support or reinforcement, it is unlikely that she will try to change very much of her behavior—especially if she has been successful with the old behaviors.

John Pickering and Robert Matson have been conducting leadership development programs for government agencies and corporations for more than twenty years. They summarize the problem in this way:

> A typical scenario emerges. After the program, participants—charged up by their experience and with a new readiness to risk change—re-enter powerful organizational environments and cultures that are exactly the same as those they left a few weeks earlier. Because no one else from the organization was exposed to it, the executives get little reinforcement of their developmental experience. Any notions of individual and organizational change they picked up in the program are knocked out of their heads by the unrelenting stress of everyday issues and problems (both personal and organizational).[8]

A leadership program, to be most effective, must be related to the participants' organizational context—before, during, and after the programs.

Limitation of Methods

Most public leadership programs use only one of four approaches (personal growth, conceptual understanding, feedback, skill building). According to Conger, the choice of method typically reflects the backgrounds and biases of the program's creators. But becoming a leader really requires more than a single approach—it requires elements of them all, and more.

Leadership skills cannot be learned in a single dose. People need time to learn new skills, to test them out, and to refine them before they become part of their repertoire. This requires a *variety* of developmental experiences, where people can safely try out new leadership techniques and get feedback and coaching to help them define and sharpen their personal leadership style.

Leaders are not trained, they are developed. And their development requires a comprehensive, balanced approach, along with sufficient time to acquire, test, and refine new skills and attitudes.

A BALANCED APPROACH
TO LEADERSHIP DEVELOPMENT

A balanced approach to leadership development contains three major elements:

- Mentoring and coaching.
- Leadership education and training.
- A series of developmental activities.

This balanced approach is not a one-shot, intensive effort, but takes two years or more for a complete cycle. It is appropriate to leaders at all levels of the organization, from the shop floor through the executive suite. While the nature of the training and of the specific development activities will be different for individuals at different levels of the organization, the balance of the three major groups of activities remains the same.

Mentoring and Coaching

The roles of mentor and coach differ in several ways. The mentor acts as a counselor to a potential leader, providing advice on career paths, development opportunities, and an overview of what it takes to become a leader in the organization. The coach is more a tutor, observing the potential leader's work and actions, providing comments on execution, and teaching skills which may be lacking. This is a key missing element in the development of managers, one that a weeklong leadership education program can never realistically be expected to provide.

Mentors are typically senior managers, at least one or two levels higher in the company than the person being mentored. The mentor must have broader experience in the company and the ability to place the leadership candidate into assignments that will help with her development. A critical element in the mentoring relationship is a mutual respect between the individual and her mentor.

Coaches, on the other hand, can come from many sources. A coach can be a colleague, a manager, or an employee. And a coach does not have to come from the same function or division. For example, a coach may come from the company's personnel or training and development function. For high-level executives, a CEO, for example, the coach may be external to the company—a peer from another corporation or a paid consultant. It is critical in the coaching relationship for the coach to have opportunities to observe an individual's work and for the individual to respect the coach and be open to feedback.

Both mentoring and coaching must be viewed as long-term relationships—a commitment of two years should be obtained before the relationship has a hope of becoming established.

These two roles, whether performed by one person or two, are an essential ingredient in the development of leaders. No matter how much education and training a person receives, and no matter how excellent that instruction may be, the incorporation of new skills and knowledge into one's work takes time, practice, and feedback. The mentor provides guidance and opportunities for practice. The coach observes and critiques the performance.

Leadership Education and Training

Leadership instruction, the second element in the leadership development model, is phased in along with ongoing mentoring/coaching and development activities. The phased approach to leadership instruction includes a series of seminars and workshops covering all four approaches (personal growth, conceptual understanding, feedback, and skill building), given over the two-year period.

The "conceptual understanding" seminar comes first in the series. This helps leadership candidates understand what it means to be a leader and what it will take to reach that goal. This seminar helps candidates assess whether they have what it takes to be a leader and whether leadership is a role they want to strive for.

Second in the series is the "personal growth" approach, which helps participants to meet and overcome their personal barriers to growth, as well as aiding them in attaining the self-confidence required of all leaders.

Skill building, the third element, includes a series of seminars and workshops that focus on specific leadership skills. Interspersed with these workshops are development activities that allow candidates to test those skills. Feedback opportunities (the fourth approach) are provided periodically by the candidates' managers, peers, and employees, and on a regular basis by their coaches.

In large organizations, where there is a constant need to develop numerous leaders, most leadership instruction will be done within the company, utilizing both internal and external resources. This allows the content of each seminar or workshop to be tailored to the organization's culture and specific issues. It also allows the scheduling of programs at the organization's convenience. At the same time, it is important to allow each leadership candidate an opportunity to attend at least one public, open-enrollment leadership seminar. This type of experience can be invaluable to the individual, allowing him to see what others are doing, to share ideas outside his own organization, and perhaps to bring back some new ideas from others.

In small organizations, where there are not sufficient numbers of leadership candidates to allow for in-house leadership instruction, it will be necessary to rely on outside programs. There are many excellent programs on the market, but content, quality, and focus vary widely. Research is necessary before sending any leadership candidate off to a program. A proper leadership development plan for even the smallest company includes all three elements and ties the mentor/coach and the development activities closely to any external leadership education.

Leadership Development Activities

Leadership candidates need regular opportunities to test and practice their leadership skills. Practice can come with regular job duties—as candidates develop these skills, their job performance should improve. But candidates also need other opportunities within which they can develop their leadership skills. Development activities can cover a wide range of assignments, ranging from ad hoc team assignments to job rotation to heading the annual United Way campaign.[9]

It is the role of the mentor, along with the candidate's manager, to provide these development opportunities, while the coach observes and critiques the candidate's performance in each situation.

Developing Your Leadership Program

The three elements, taken together, provide a comprehensive approach to leadership development. The two-year cycle for the program allows sufficient time to provide the instruction, practice, and feedback necessary to do the job fully and well.

It is important to note that instruction must be provided not only to the leadership candidates themselves, but also to their mentors and coaches. Being a mentor or a coach is a different role from being a manager and involves different sets of skills. Assigning people to those roles without properly preparing them is a certain way to sink a leadership program before it is even launched.

Organizations that are starting leadership development programs need to examine the options available to them, both on the open market and through in-house development, and choose specific topics and approaches that match their organizational culture and context.

LEADERSHIP DEVELOPMENT AT NYPRO

NYPRO, headquartered in Clinton, Massachusetts, has an interesting approach to leadership development. Its leadership development program includes three elements:

- An annual general managers' meeting.

- The NYPRO Leadership Institute, run four times a year.

- The use of internal boards of directors for each of its twenty worldwide companies and joint ventures.

Because the company consists of many small plants scattered around the world, there are few opportunities for the various corporate and plant managers to meet as a group. Their annual general managers' meeting provides this opportunity. The location of the meeting rotates, being hosted by one plant in cooperation with a local university.

The general managers' meeting has three major components:

- An opportunity for the CEO and corporate management to update the plant managers on new directions and strategic initiatives.

- An educational component, provided by a cooperating university (this year focusing on how to build teamwork).

- A full day designed by the plant managers themselves where they can benchmark against other NYPRO plants and learn from each other.

The other two activities are targeted at up-and-coming leaders. The NYPRO Leadership Institute, most recently developed with the Worcester Polytechnic Institute, targets mid-level managers and focuses on using a variety of leadership learning methods. This year's program included sessions on creative problem solving, dealing with organizational change, leadership, strategic thinking, and a team-building exercise (a ropes course). Instructors included NYPRO managers, college faculty, and external consultants. The NYPRO Leadership Institute supplements other management development programs given within the company or which employees take at local colleges and universities.

The most unique leadership development activity at NYPRO is the use of "internal boards of directors" for each of its operations. According to CEO Gordon Lankton, each board has from three to six members from *middle* management. They are appointed annually based on their leadership potential and their background (to represent a variety of functional areas). Each board runs the local business, according to Lankton, including the "hiring and firing of the general manager." They make operational and capital decisions, needing to get corporate approval only in extreme cases, such as "when they want to fire the general manager or have an extremely large capital expenditure." NYPRO's leadership development program is an excellent example of a balanced approach to leadership development by a medium-sized company.

KEY POINTS

There is a set of seven leadership practices that forms the first foundation for the learning organization. If present, they provide a firm footing for the journey to organizational transformation. Their absence makes it all too easy for the superstructure of high-level skills to collapse on itself.

Leaders exist in all parts and at all levels of the organization, and all must be properly prepared for their roles in the transformation effort. Their development requires a combination of mentoring, coaching, and a variety of developmental activities along with more traditional instructional methods.

In building this first foundation, to ensure that leaders are ready to shepherd your company's revolution, you need to keep in mind three key points.

1. There is no single formula for the development of leaders for the learning organization.
2. Any development effort must be tailored to each organization's culture and context.
3. Taking the time to build this foundation will help ensure the success of the learning organization.

THREE

THE "THINKING" LITERACY CHALLENGE

- A steelworker misorders $1 million in parts because he cannot read well.

- An insurance clerk who doesn't understand decimals pays a claimant $2,200 instead of $22.

- A manufacturing technician unable to read assembly instructions nearly kills several of his co-workers by incorrectly fitting a heavy piece of equipment onto a machine.[1]

The U.S. Department of Education estimates that some 27 million Americans are "functionally illiterate," encompassing 30 percent of all unskilled workers, 29 percent of semiskilled workers, and 11 percent of all managers, professionals, and technicians. As shocking as these numbers are, they are based on a long-standing definition of "functional literacy," which involves the most minimal of capabilities:

- Reading skills: ability to read a newspaper.

- Writing skills: ability to fill out a job application.

- Mathematical skills: ability to count your change at the supermarket.

With 27 million Americans functionally illiterate, and another 45 million "marginally" illiterate, the challenge to the educational system and to employers is overwhelming. The problem becomes even greater when one considers that the basic skills needed by workers in a twenty-first century corporation will go far beyond the standard definition of "functional literacy."

> In her book, *In the Age of the Smart Machine*, Shoshanna Zuboff talks about "informating" a paper mill. Workers who once judged the efficiency of a factory process by how the static electricity from the machinery affected their hair now sit in an environmentally controlled command center and monitor the same processes by reading graphs and numbers on a computer terminal.

The learning organization cannot succeed unless every employee possesses basic skills that go far beyond the standard definition of functional literacy. In today's competitive climate, employees and their knowledge are the organization's competitive edge. As Anthony Carnevale, executive director of the Institute for Workplace Learning, points out:

> As technology becomes more abundant and instantaneously available worldwide, employees' skills become an employer's competitive edge. The workplace now demands that workers have more than just a good command of the three Rs. Employers want and need workers with a broad set of workplace skills—or at least with a strong foundation of basics that facilitates learning on the job.[2]

I call these new requirements not "functional" literacy, but "thinking" literacy, for the ability to think and reason is a basic requirement for the learning organization. "Thinking" literacy includes:

- Communication skills.

- Mathematical skills.

- Self-management skills.

- Business skills.

- Team skills.

- Function-specific skills.

Draftsmen and model makers seldom have drawing boards or modeling materials any longer. They must rely on two- and three-dimensional representations of their work on a computer screen. Rather than picking up a pen and ruler or a curved knife to make changes in their work, they must enter commands on a keyboard and let the computer change the image on the screen.

COMMUNICATIONS SKILLS

In today's work environment, few employees work in isolation. The old stereotype of the worker, typified by Charlie Chaplin in his film *Modern Times*, who spends his career tightening the same bolts on products coming down the assembly line is no longer a realistic portrayal of life in the modern organization. Because employees must work together, they must communicate with each other. These interactions involve both in-bound and out-bound communications and require a comprehensive set of communications skills.

Language

Given the composition of America's workforce today, and projections of its composition at the end of this century, it is clear that many workers will have a native language other than English. Depending on the content of specific jobs, there may be a requirement for workers to learn English and to be able to communicate in English at the appropriate levels (see below), or for supervisors and managers to learn other languages.

> The Marriott Corporation examined the composition of its workforce for one division of its food business, and tried to predict what the composition would likely be over the next decade. Based on this study, Marriott now requires that all first-line supervisors be able to speak Spanish, and offers Berlitz Spanish instruction to its employees.[3]

At the same time, many employers are now finding it necessary to sponsor "English as a Second Language" classes for their employees. Whether they speak English, Spanish, or other languages, there is a need for employees to learn to use language properly, to rid themselves of street language and other poor speaking and writing habits.

> As long as a half-century ago, Caterpillar introduced a workshop for supervisors called "Better English." As told by L. J. Fletcher, manager of Caterpillar training programs until his retirement in 1956: "The foremen will speak the language of the shop. Men who talk to him about their work use the language they wish to use which sometimes is quite expressive, sometimes quite profane and, . . . many terms which are incorrect. . . . [The instructor] was able to pick out a number of the more common mistakes . . . and then emphasize the correct usage that they should employ. We did not particularly say to these men that later on, as

they might progress in the company, there would come a time they would be talking to others, maybe representing Caterpillar at various meetings. If they still employed these rather glaring mistakes, it would not be to the advantage of either the individual or the company."[4]

Often, when testing employees for other skills, such as mathematical expertise, companies discover that some employees score poorly not because the employees cannot do the math, but because they cannot read the questions.

Reading

Whether reading interoffice memos, customer letters, equipment instruction manuals, or any other type of work-related material, today's employee must be able to read at a minimum of a *tenth-grade* level. This level of reading capability exceeds the standard definition of "functional literacy," but it is necessary for survival in today's and tomorrow's corporation.

Many major employers, for at least the past three decades, have preferred to hire someone holding a high school equivalency certificate rather than a person with a high school diploma. The reason: The equivalency certificate guarantees that the holder can read, write, and do arithmetic at a sixth-grade level; the high school diploma carries no such guarantee.

Specific jobs may carry an even higher requirement for reading proficiency, depending on the reading level of the materials needed to perform the job and the percentage of technical content.

Listening

Along with reading, it is also necessary for employees to understand the spoken word. Listening skills involve not only understanding the words that are actually spoken, but also include the ability to "read" body language and tone of voice—to hear what is being said "between the lines."

> An organizational development consultant was invited to sit in on a product development meeting involving twenty design and manufacturing engineers and their managers. The meeting plodded along, with each group giving its report and recommendations, and others nodding agreement. After about an hour of observation, the consultant interrupted the meeting: "You're not listening to each other. You're not getting to the real issues. Your heads are nodding yes, but your body language is screaming NO!!!" The meeting participants told the consultant that he didn't know what he was talking about, and continued through their agenda.
>
> An hour later, the consultant interrupted again and repeated his message. Again, he was told to sit down and be quiet. Just before lunch, he spoke up for the third time. This time, one of the engineers spoke up: "You're right. I think they are full of !@$#, but I wasn't brave enough to say anything."
>
> This one comment broke the logjam of emotions and allowed the real issues to come to the fore. By the end of the day, with the help of the consultant, the group had made a start on better communications and, as a result, a better product development plan.

Writing

Written communications, both on paper and via electronic media, are a necessary part of corporate life. Writing skills involve being able to express oneself clearly, to ensure clear communications. "Business Writing" has become a very popular course in many organizations, where, even though employees have basic writing skills, company memos and reports have suffered from too much jargon, unclear language, and general overflow. Some companies even have started handwriting programs to improve the legibility of employees' script. Unless one's written communications are comprehensible, misunderstandings and errors will occur.

> My wife, an occupational therapist who works in a public school system, was asked to help a fireman improve his handwriting. The young man was a graduate of the local high school and did his job well as one of the department's paramedics, but was in danger of losing his job because his superiors could not read his handwritten reports. They feared that someone might misread a symptom or treatment on one of the reports and make a fatal error in treating a patient.

Speaking

Not every employee in an organization must become a proficient orator, capable of making a professional presentation to the public or press, but every employee *must* have basic speaking skills. Surveys regularly show that "fear of public speaking" is the most widespread phobia in the populace. Basic instruction on speaking skills helps employees be better understood and enables them to overcome this fear. It also empowers them to contribute their knowledge and ideas to discussions of problems. Too often, good ideas are lost because employees are not confident that they will be able to express themselves well, and so they withhold their ideas in group discussions.

> In the mid-1980s, I was responsible for a series of public seminars that my company offered to its customers. A number of the presenters in these seminars were engineers. I insisted that all of the seminar speakers take a presentation skills workshop. Many of the engineers fought the idea, believing that all that mattered was their ease with the subject matter—they felt that their expertise would become apparent to customers and would more than compensate for any lack of polish in their speaking. Several years later, I met two of the engineers who had been forced to take the training. They said that the skills they had acquired through the workshop were in great part responsible for the promotions they recently had received.

MATHEMATICAL SKILLS

> Motorola, in planning to introduce new product technologies to its Arlington Heights plant, tested its workers for basic mathematical skills. According to William Wiggenhorn, corporate vice president for training and education and president of Motorola University, "Only 40% passed a test containing some questions as simple as 'Ten is what percent of 100?' "[5]

The level of mathematical skills required is a function of the employee's job. But, even so, the case can be made that all employees should have more than just basic arithmetical skills—that basic algebra is required. In the era of Statistical Process Control, of "informating" processes, it is necessary for employees to be able to read and interpret at least basic two-axis graphs, and this requires basic algebra. Higher levels of skills may be required, depending on job content (see "Function-Specific Skills" section on pages 67–68).

When I first graduated from college, I spent several years teaching math at the junior high school level. It became apparent that some students couldn't tell time. Yet there was nothing in the junior high curriculum on this subject. Children are taught to tell time in the second grade. If students didn't grasp the concepts and develop the skills then, they were lost—the skills were never repeated in higher grades.

No matter what the causes of employees' math deficiencies, mathematical skills are now an integral part of most people's jobs. Even if they rely on a computer or a calculator to do most mathematical figuring, people need to understand basic math concepts, to know how to set up a problem for their electronic helpers, and to have a sense of when an answer provided by those helpers does or doesn't make sense.

SELF-MANAGEMENT SKILLS

No matter how much instruction is provided by an organization, the primary responsibility for all learning lies with the individual. The individual must master three key skills:

- How to learn.

- How to reason.

- How to plan his or her own life and career.

Learning to Learn

The ability to learn relates to the ability to solve problems, master change, and face uncertainty. If a person knows how to learn, she will be able to cope with new situations. Learning to learn is not a course on study skills or how to use a library, but it may include those skills. Basically, it tells how to plan a course of action that will lead to mastery of a new situation.

> The Parker Bertea Aerospace Group, in trying to validate a simple test of math skills for use in screening new employees, discovered that many of their current employees were deficient in these skills. How were these employees doing their jobs so well, given this lack of basic skills? They relied on calculators, on machine gauges, and on the assistance of others in the group who they knew had the math skills. In other words, while many of the employees had not learned basic math skills, they had learned how to get their jobs done. When shown how to use gauges and tools to make adjustments to the production or to test machinery, they made physical marks on them as guides for the future.[6]

People learn how to learn by experiencing the process. This may sound redundant, but what it means is that the best way of teaching someone to learn is to guide the person's learning (in a basic problem-solving course, for example), making certain that the person pays attention not only to the subject matter, but also to the process she is using to learn the subject matter.

Learning is a self-reinforcing activity. People who say, "I'm too old to learn" or "I was never a good student, I can't learn" need to be guided through the learning process and shown explicitly what they have learned already. Once an employee realizes that he can learn, he can then step back to examine how he has learned, so that he can repeat the learning sequence again in the future.

People's learning styles vary. Some learn best by reading, some by being shown, some by doing it themselves. Each student must find the right method for himself.

Learning to Reason

Learning to reason is akin to learning to learn. It is a process of structuring problems and following a logical procedure to solve those problems. The subject may be taught as a "Problem Solving and Decision Making" workshop or can be the subject of coaching by a supervisor: "How do you think you should analyze and solve this problem?"

> At Blount Canada Ltd., employees being taught Statistical Process Control are intentionally *not* given computer-based tools to generate the statistics on their work processes. According to Blount's Eugene Kraemer: "They need to understand the process, so we make them do the calculations by hand. In this way, they understand where the data is coming from, how it is being handled, and what the resulting charts mean. They can then better judge what they need to do to improve or fix their processes."

Training in reasoning skills empowers employees to understand better exactly what they are doing and shows them how they can improve their work processes themselves. Blount's quality manager, Dan Lawson, told me that it is the operators and mechanics who improve the processes in the factory: "Two percent here, five percent there—it all adds up. We're improving overall factory productivity eight to ten percent per year, and it's the people on the floor who are doing it."

Life/Career Planning Skills

There are few companies today that can offer guarantees of lifetime employment. Economic conditions are forcing layoffs in almost every industry, from automobiles to computers to banking.

Employees, fearful of losing their jobs, suffer such high levels of anxiety that they often cannot focus properly on their work.

> Anthony Carnevale, executive director of the Institute for Workplace Learning, says in *Workplace Basics*: "Organizations traditionally have viewed *self-esteem, motivation, goal setting,* and *employability/career development* as skills an individual should acquire outside the workplace. But the demands of today's evolving workplace are influencing employers to recognize that when workers do not have these skills, organizations must provide training opportunities to build them."[7]

Equipping people with basic skills, along with self-awareness and career planning training, allows them to be more self-confident, productive employees. These programs can help employees feel that even if they cannot rely on their current employer for lifetime employment, they are, indeed, employable elsewhere. This reduces anxiety and helps people focus on their roles. One worker at Northern Telecom's Bramalea plant expressed it this way:

> "I am [taking all of this training] not only because it is my job but I am doing it for me. The company is becoming flatter and there is not that much room at the top for all of us to be promoted. I have got to rely on making my own job more interesting and rewarding. . . . With each new training, each new project, I feel that I am securing my job—maybe not in this company forever—but in the job market out there."[8]

BUSINESS SKILLS

Employees need to understand the business their organization is in and how their work contributes toward the success of that business. Thus employees come to realize that their work makes a difference and contributes toward overall organizational goals.

> Springfield Remanufacturing Corporation is an engine re-builder in Missouri. CEO Jack Stack, to give all employees knowledge of the company's business, invented a game known as the Great Game of Business. As reported in *Inc.* magazine: "Employees are trained to understand every detail of the company's financials. Every quarter they get bonuses pegged to goals such as return on assets. In the meantime they play the game: watching weekly income statements and cash-flow reports, comparing projected figures with actual."[9]

Profit and loss are only vague concepts to most employees in American industry. They know that profits are good and losses are bad, but they don't know how their individual performance fits into the company's financial results. So employees focus on their own performance measures, defined by their professions, their job descriptions, and their managers. Too often, they find themselves working in a manner that while optimizing their individual objectives, may be suboptimizing the overall company's business results. Knowledge of basic business information empowers employees to make decisions to help their companies succeed.

TEAM SKILLS

Most of the transformation programs being tried by American industry include teamwork as a major component. Whether a company is pursuing the learning organization, TQM, or other initiatives, teams play a critical role. The types of teams range from quality circles on the factory floor to cross-functional new product development teams to cross-company quality improvement teams involving major segments of a company's supply chain.

Working effectively on a team requires skills that build on, but differ from, the other basic skills under discussion. These include:

- Becoming an effective team player.

- Meeting skills.

- Negotiations skills.

Becoming an Effective Team Player

American society has always prized individual achievement and has stressed the importance of the *individual*. The only knowledge most people growing up in our society have of the concept of "teamwork" is from team sports, which many citizens never experience themselves. Thus, in order to foster effective teamwork, organizations must sometimes educate their people about what teamwork means, what roles people play on teams, and how to become an effective team player.

Meeting Skills

A lot of the work of teams is done in meetings. To make these meetings productive means that they must be planned and managed effectively. This requires a set of skills for meeting managers, facilitators, and participants, including:

- Knowing when a meeting is or isn't necessary.

- Planning an agenda.

- Determining who needs to attend.

- Managing a meeting.

- Ensuring that necessary decisions are actually made during the meeting.

- Ensuring that action items taken are actually done.

- Ensuring that all meeting attendees participate.

- Negotiating and resolving conflict (discussed below).

Negotiations Skills

A cross-functional team will, at first, almost always find its members working at cross-purposes. The different functions represented on the team all have their own goals and standards for their work. To optimize the overall work of the team means, almost by definition, that various groups represented on the team cannot each win every argument. Negotiations are needed to find the best solution for any problem. All team members must be trained in negotiations skills to keep them on an equal footing, and to help the team reach the optimal solutions they seek.

FUNCTION-SPECIFIC SKILLS

All of the above basic skill sets can be thought of as "generic," that is, they are required of all employees, regardless of job function or level. In addition to these basic skills, there will also be some function-specific skills required of employees. Electronics technicians, whether building, testing, or servicing equipment, need basic knowledge of electronic principles as well as skills in diagnosing problems, using test equipment, etc. Customer service operators need skills in customer relations, using the company's telephone and order entry systems, etc. Salespeople need basic sales skills, including prospecting, negotiating, closing, etc.

The basic skills needed by any employee will be a combination of the generic skills described in this chapter and the requirements of her specific job.

Robert Fowler, president of Hampden Papers in Holyoke, Massachusetts, describes the changing role of factory workers in his paper mill: "There used to be a time when we had people working here who were functionally illiterate. We had plenty of jobs for them. But today we don't have jobs like that, not a single one. . . . We used to have a machine . . . that produced 1500 lineal feet of paper a day. At that rate, we could say to the operator, 'Push the green button in the morning, the red button in the afternoon, and call us if you need help.' . . . [The new machines] produce enormously more per man hour, but they also require a great deal more from the machine operator per man hour. At one time, if the man did it wrong the penalty was that he spoiled two reams of paper. Now if he does it wrong he spoils enough paper to stretch the entire length of Massachusetts."[10]

ACQUIRING BASIC SKILLS

The learning organization cannot be established if a company has a deficit of basic skills at any level. The ideal way for a company to ensure that all employees have basic skills is to screen applicants before they are hired. This, however, will solve the total problem only if a company is starting with a greenfield operation, staffing the entire operation from scratch. Even then, experience shows that the company cannot assume there are sufficient numbers of applicants in the labor pool who have the full complement of basic skills.

Motorola, in screening applicants for jobs in its Arlington Heights cellular telephone manufacturing plant, found only one of forty-seven applicants who could pass the basic skills test and a drug test.[11]

The fact is that American industry is facing a shrinking labor pool and an available labor pool deficient in many of the basic skills. The Bureau of Labor Statistics estimates that more than 80 percent of the people who will be employed in American industry in the next ten to fifteen years are already in the labor pool. Therefore, organizations must work to ensure that their current employees either have or attain the necessary basic skills.

> The Business Council for Effective Literacy has been reporting on "Adult Literacy Programs, Planning and Issues" for the past decade. There has been an interesting trend in the section of their quarterly newsletter titled "Corporate Literacy Action" over the past several years. Up until about 1990, most of the items they reported were about companies' donations to local literacy programs through public schools, colleges, or voluntary organizations. It is only in the last several years that many companies have realized that they have substantial literacy problems within their existing workforce and have started implementing in-house programs for their own employees.

This does not mean that companies have to develop and deliver this instruction themselves. There are many resources in virtually every American community to help employers train their people. Public school systems have programs with titles like "English as a Second Language" and "Adult Basic Education." Community colleges throughout the country are charged with the responsibility for developing their communities' labor supply, and they provide developmental education to build basic skills. Labor unions and professional societies are addressing the problem of basic skills through educational programs targeted at their respective memberships. Voluntary community agencies sponsor adult literacy programs. The resources, while not endless, are sufficiently plentiful that no organization should feel it has to do the job alone.

> The Finger Lakes Regional Education Center for Economic Development is a consortium of education providers, including public school systems and two- and four-year

colleges, covering a wide area in Upstate New York. They have developed a modular curriculum covering basic skills as well as Statistical Process Control, problem solving, decision making, and basic computer skills. The modular design of the curriculum materials makes them easily transportable and usable by employers ranging from Eastman Kodak with its forty-six thousand employees to small machine tool companies with fewer than fifty employees. Similar programs, whether developed by a single school system or college or by a similar consortium, are available in every state.

RELATING BASIC SKILLS TO THE JOB

Many employees will resist the idea of basic skills training. "I've been doing my job well for the past ten years. Why are you now telling me that I need better math skills? What's wrong with my work? Just leave me alone . . . I'm doing fine."

People must be presented with basic skills training as part of their career development and job security strategy. Technologies are changing at an ever-increasing pace. More and more, rote work is being handled by machines, making the work of people ever more complicated. Basic skills are needed to keep up with the pace of change. Without basic skills, employees' work can easily be made obsolete.

To make the basic skills training more interesting and relevant to employees, it should be related to the company's real work. Whatever you are teaching, there are prime opportunities to have employees relate what they are learning directly to their jobs. This will not only make the material more interesting and relevant to the students, but will also result in more immediate increases in productivity based on the newly acquired skills. Are you teaching English as a Second Language? Use the manuals for the employees' computer terminals as course material. Are you teaching mathematical skills? Use quality charts from the factory floor to explain two-dimensional graphs. Are you teaching problem-solving skills? Use an example of how to reduce time for a machine setup.

Basic skills training is a necessity for large companies and small. The two following examples of basic skills programs—from NYPRO and the American Transportation Company (AMTRAN)—illustrate how this training is applied.

NYPRO

The town of Clinton, Massachusetts, the local source for NYPRO employees, has had an increasing population of foreign immigrants in recent years. As a result, NYPRO sponsors "English as a Second Language" courses at its Clinton plant. While the course is given by external faculty, it uses materials from NYPRO—machine instructions, employee handbooks, etc.—for the English reading materials. This makes the course immediately relevant to its forty-three participants.

Remedial mathematics and English instruction are provided by a local community college. NYPRO thought that its employees might not be attracted to a course that included "remedial" as part of its title. It therefore worked with the staff at Quinsigamond Community College to develop a "Tech-Prep" course to help unskilled workers prepare for more skilled work.

NYPRO Clinton president Brian Jones feels that the company's investment in training and development has been in large part responsible for the lowering of employee turnover in the plant, from an annual rate of more than 100% in 1985 to less than 5 percent in 1993. As he told me: "The best message you can give employees is investment in training and development—it shows respect for the individual. It also shows them that they have a future. Employees won't show enthusiasm unless the company shows interest in them."

AMERICAN TRANSPORTATION COMPANY

AmTran is a major American bus manufacturer. Located in Conway, Arkansas, it has a work force of 850. Today's manufacturing processes and procedures require higher levels of basic skills and computer literacy than ever before. Because of these changes, AmTran asked the Conway Adult Learning Center to assess both its workers' skills and the skills needed for the various jobs in the plant. In April 1988, based on the assessment results, the Adult Learning Center started offering on-site basic skills courses on math and reading. Since then, the curriculum has been expanded to include strands built around specific job needs, such as blueprint reading, office procedures, and computer skills.

AmTran employees participate voluntarily, attending one hour, twice a week, during work hours. "You can see improvement in line and job performance and in switching over to the new systems," notes Lennie Whiteman, AmTran's program coordinator. "The workers also feel much better about their jobs and themselves."[12]

KEY POINTS

"Thinking" literacy, the second foundation for the learning organization, surpasses what is commonly known as "functional" literacy, and encompasses a set of basic skills that all employees must master to enable the learning organization. Ranging from the three Rs to business, team, and self-management skills, all are prerequisites to the major transformation efforts many organizations are starting in order to compete effectively into the twenty-first century.

Many resources are available in most communities to help organizations equip their employees to master these basic skills, so companies do not have to feel that they must develop and deliver all of the needed education and training themselves. The role of the company is to (1) clearly identify the skills needed by employees at all levels, (2) identify skills deficits in their employees, (3) recruit local resources to provide the needed instruction, and (4) help those resources tailor the programs using company-specific materials and examples.

FOUR

OVERCOMING FUNCTIONAL MYOPIA

During the course of building a new house some years ago, I happened to stop by the site one afternoon. As I walked through the house, I found the drywall contractor finishing his work in what would be the dining room. He had done a fine job, except for one thing—the insulation contractor had not yet insulated the walls.

"What do you think you're doing?" I asked.

"I'm doing what I'm paid to do—put up drywall."

"But the insulation isn't in the walls yet!" I complained.

"That's not my problem," he replied. "I'm being paid to do the drywall."

This contractor measured his work by how good a job he did on the drywall, whether the work was done on time, and whether he made his profit. In doing his job, he did not consider how his work fit into the overall plans for the house—he didn't care whether the walls were insulated or not.

Similarly, in high-technology companies, design engineers

traditionally measure their work by the elegance of their designs, whether the design of a new product has all of the latest bells and whistles. Their product designs may win industry awards for their elegance and state-of-the-art components, but if a product is not what the customer wants, if it is loaded with features that raise costs but that few customers will ever use, there is little point to the design exercise.

"Functional myopia" exists when an organization—or a person—becomes so focused on its local or group goals and standards that it loses sight of the overall goals of the company. No individual or group is exempt from this syndrome, from the petty-cash clerk to the legal department to the engineering manager to the division manager to the drywall contractor. I'm sure that you have experienced, and been frustrated by, the functional myopia of many people and groups you deal with daily in your personal and professional lives.

The learning organization cannot succeed where functional myopia is widespread. In the learning organization, people learn from each other, regardless of level or function. Functional myopia makes this kind of learning, the sharing of information and ideas, difficult if not impossible.

THE COSTS OF FUNCTIONAL MYOPIA

Functional myopia can cause the overall goals of a company not to be maximized or, at worst, not to be reached at all. In the case of my house, if I had not happened to visit it that day, I would not have known that the dining room wasn't insulated until the following winter, when I investigated why the room was so cold. In the case of the high-tech manufacturer, the myopia of design engineers often results in products that customers don't want or that are priced so high they are noncompetitive in the market. Functional myopia can subvert the best-laid plans of any organization.

- The purchasing department, in seeking the lowest-cost supplier (its traditional measure of performance), may overlook product quality or timeliness of delivery, thereby foiling the company's attempts to improve quality or reduce time to market.

- The materials manager in one factory may hoard a key material so that it is always in stock locally, even while another of the company's factories may have to shut down for several weeks because of a shortage of that key material.

- The legal department may hold up a key industry alliance because of battles over minor wording changes in the partnership agreement.

- The training department may stall sales of a new product by sticking so rigorously to its standards for course development that training is not available on the product for six months after the product is ready.

The list of ways in which functional myopia can hurt organizations is endless. But if everyone is working for the same company, how does functional myopia happen?

THE ROOTS OF FUNCTIONAL MYOPIA

New companies don't suffer from functional myopia. In a start-up company, there is a small group of entrepreneurs who work together constantly with a united purpose—to develop that first product or service and sell it.

But as the start-up grows, the small group of entrepreneurs expands, and with that expansion typically comes functional specialization. As each function expands, departments become larger and the focus tends to narrow to the work of the department, with employees often losing sight of the company's overall goals. Research, design, manufacture, marketing, and service become sequential activities, with each department waiting for the previous department to finish its work before passing it on.

It is unclear exactly when in the growth of a company this begins to happen. Research has shown that employees separated by a relatively small distance—those on different floors of the same building or by more than six offices on the same floor—tend not to communicate with each other. It may be this lack of communication, more than any other factor, that accounts for functional myopia.

This "throw it over the wall" method of work flow creates its own problems. Often, design engineers create a new product and pass the completed design on to manufacturing, only to have the manufacturing department return it weeks later with the message: "It's a wonderful product and a beautiful design. There's only one problem: It can't be built the way you designed it—at least not for the price customers are willing to pay." Or, similarly, a product will be manufactured only to find out that servicing it is next to impossible.

Every function has its share of functional myopia, from purchasing to legal to manufacturing to sales. No one is exempt. Even top managers in an organization tend to carry the functional biases from the groups in which they originally served. Functional myopia stems from three primary roots: cultural, organizational, and administrative.

Cultural Roots

Cultural issues, dealing with the norms of behavior for the overall corporation and for individual functions and organizations within the company, can take many forms. They may appear as stereotypes of various functions: one function may refer to members of another as "prima donnas" or "tool jockeys" or other, usually disparaging nicknames. Similar stereotypes often exist between labor and management. Some are traceable to long-standing rivalries, others to actual differences in status as reflected in salary scales and perquisites, such as office size.

> In one high-tech company, the union representative tersely stated the union's position on work teams: "The union is against work teams." When asked why the union held this view, he cited one example: The company had put together a work team in one area of the plant, and the team "had reduced the work from four days to four hours. What happened to the rest of the work?" he asked. "The union's job is to preserve jobs."

Each profession has its own standards by which it measures the quality of its work. At the most simplistic level, one could say that design engineers are measured on the elegance and performance of their designs, manufacturing engineers on how inexpensively a product can be made, service engineers on "mean time to repair" (MTTR), purchasing people on getting the lowest prices from suppliers, etc. These goals, which are closely tied to individuals' performance measures and reward systems, are often in conflict with each other. For example, a design feature may boost performance but also increase manufacturing cost, or a certain method of manufacture may lower production costs but increase servicing costs. Resolution of such conflicts cannot always be made on the basis of "objective" technical criteria. More often, it is a "political" process (politics being defined as "the art of the possible").

> Digital Equipment Corporation's Telecommunications and Networks Group realized several years ago that its elegant designs of local area network (LAN) components were pricing the products out of the market. While a small proportion of their customer base (the most technically sophisticated customers) liked all of the "bells and whistles" in Digital's LAN products, most of the market was looking

for inexpensive, reliable, "vanilla-flavored" solutions. To better meet market demands, the engineering group had to overcome their functional myopia (that design excellence was its own reward). According to the group manufacturing manager, Bill Burke, "The engineering standard for design of LAN components moved from state of the *art* to state of the *shelf*"—meaning that designers would, as much as possible, use current manufacturing practices and components in their product designs in order to reduce manufacturing costs and produce a more competitive product.

Organizational Roots

Many manufacturing companies have grown up as hierarchies in which each function has its own department, and communications between the functions take place primarily at the tops of the respective departments—the vice presidents of engineering and manufacturing meet regularly to discuss issues, but managers and individual contributors lower in their groups don't often confer. These commonly are called "stovepipe" organizations.

Because members of each organization cannot see beyond their respective stovepipes, their focus is local or myopic. To succeed, they must adhere to the standards and practices of their respective functions. Even if they thought that there would be some benefit to the company from working more closely with their counterparts in other functions, the boundaries of their respective stovepipes bar this from happening. "Just do your own work and let the other department worry about theirs."

Working as manager of education and training for Digital Equipment Corporation's Networks and Communications Marketing Group, I was responsible for ensuring that field-based sales and sales support personnel had the training they needed to sell our products and services. My job was separate from Digital's educational services organization, which had its own departments for sales and sales support training.

My group had developed a one-day seminar to prepare the field for the introduction of a new product. The training, done once for a limited audience, had been well received. After the first session, many requests came from various field locations to repeat the training. I went to the educational services organization and asked them to take our materials, polish them, and start offering the workshop to field audiences.

"That's not the way we work," I was told. If I wanted them to provide this training to the field, they would have to follow their in-house procedures: a needs assessment, development of course objectives, research into the subject matter, development and testing of materials, etc. It would take twelve months and cost between $50,000 and $80,000. If I funded them, they might even be able to compress the schedule and start offering the training in nine months.

The educational services organization could not see beyond its own stovepipe. They had, for many years, worked according to a very strict set of rules, and they had been successful by their own measures: they regularly won industry awards for the excellence of their training materials. But they could not concern themselves with pressing training needs or with how they could better meet overall company goals by using materials that were developed by people outside their own organization who didn't follow their strict guidelines for instructional development.

Administrative Roots

American society has frequently looked to the individual as a source of heroism. This is reflected in our school systems, our folklore (from Davy Crockett to John Wayne to Ross Perot), and our general upbringing. It is also reflected in the way measurement and reward systems are generally structured in American industry, i.e. keyed to individual achievement, rather than to effective teamwork.

Because of this individualistic orientation, as well as our tendency to develop stovepipe organizations, there are actually *disincentives* for most employees to remove their functional blinders. "If my performance and salary reviews are based on the standards and goals of my own organization, I had better make certain that I play by the rules." So trying to cooperate across functions or organizations can actually result in a poorer performance review, even if it is better for the overall goals of the company.

> Consultant Michael Hammer tells a story from the airline industry: "A plane belonging to a major American airline was grounded one afternoon for repairs at Airport A, but the nearest mechanic qualified to perform the repairs worked at Airport B. The manager at Airport B refused to send the mechanic to Airport A that afternoon, because after completing the repairs the mechanic would have had to stay overnight at a hotel, and the hotel bill would come out of B's budget. So, the mechanic was dispatched to Airport A early the following morning, which enabled him to fix the plane and return home the same day. A multi-million-dollar aircraft sat idle, and the airline lost hundreds of thousands of dollars in revenue, but Manager B's budget wasn't hit for a $100 hotel bill. Manager B was neither foolish nor careless. He was doing exactly what he was supposed to be doing: controlling and minimizing his expenses."[1]

OVERCOMING FUNCTIONAL MYOPIA

Given the root causes of functional myopia, how can organizations overcome these barriers to get employees at all levels to work together, to consider the larger picture, and to optimize overall company results, rather than individual, functional goals? Functional myopia can be overcome only by addressing all three root causes. To accomplish this, a three-pronged approach is required:

- Education and training to overcome cultural barriers and to develop cross-functional teamwork.

- Changes in organizational design to eliminate stove-pipes.

- Changes in administrative policies and procedures to tie individual measurements and rewards more closely to overall company goals.

Education and Training

Education is necessary to help employees understand how their individual work is tied to the overall goals of the organization. Games such as that developed by Springfield Remanufacturing CEO Jack Stack really do aid employees in making sense of their company's financial data. Such games and simulations can help employees understand the industry their company is part of and also how they fit into the overall business.

> Caterpillar uses a business simulation as part of a seminar to help business teams understand "the overall interaction of the various parts of a business unit and how these parts impact on one another." The simulation models an industrial market with distinct market segments and competitors. Teams select appropriate production strategies and perform financial analyses to test the results of their strategies. This program helps teams not only develop a better understanding of their business responsibilities, but also helps them develop their team working styles.

Another method of developing employees' understanding of their business is through charting and analysis of the company's business processes and value chain. As stated by Graham Palmer of Northern Telecom Canada: "An end-to-end process view of the company enables everyone to examine how work flows, how decisions are made across functions, and, most importantly, how customers relate to the total process and how they measure success."[2]

Springs Industries' Grey Manufacturing Division undertook this type of value chain analysis as part of its overall business process redesign efforts. A cross-functional team, empowered by, but not including, William K. Easley, at that time the division president, started out to analyze the company's information systems requirements. Shortly after starting the process, the task force concluded that their mission was only "to replace what was already there." But to make the quantum improvements they were seeking for the business, they concluded, they "had to ask better questions."

As a result of these discussions, they spent six months charting and analyzing the division's business processes. With the assistance of a team of consultants from Digital Equipment Corporation and two proprietary methodologies called TOP MAP and Requirements Analysis for Manufacturing Systems (RAMS)[3], the team plotted out the division's business processes, including its entire internal and cross-divisional value chain. The process began with a daylong meeting of 150 people representing that complete value chain, including key suppliers and customers within Springs's other fourteen divisions and its corporate offices.

Charles P. McJunkin, the Springs project manager, describes the benefits of the exhaustive exercise in this way: "Before we started, we really didn't know much about the whole process—how we related to each other." He says that the greatest lessons learned were that "the most powerful systems we operate are our people systems. The real return is in the work you do with the people systems." Automation and information systems can add value later in the process, he told me, but only after you align the objectives and processes of the business.

This experiment with Springs Industries' Grey Manufacturing Division was such a success that it is being emulated by other operating divisions of the company. According to Easley, the sponsor of the original experiment, the process gave Springs a whole new focus on how to improve its business processes. He believes that this exercise will make a real difference in improving the company's return on assets (ROA) and in gaining competitive advantage.

There are many excellent methodologies available in the marketplace for process charting and analysis: the "systems thinking" methodologies described by Peter Senge,[4] IDEF Modeling, originally developed for the U.S. Department of Defense, Digital's TOP MAP and RAMS, and the methodologies contained in Hammer and Champy's recent book, *Reengineering the Corporation*, among others.

Activity-Based Costing (ABC)

Another methodology that can provide insights into how the business really operates is known as Activity-Based Costing (ABC). ABC is an accounting technique used to allocate indirect costs to specific company activities or products. This methodology takes exception to the standard accounting practices for allocating overhead and other indirect expenses and requires examination of exactly how indirect costs apply. The process of investigating these costs not only allows for understanding a company's cost structure, but also requires that the company's business processes be examined, analyzed, and understood.

A major aerospace/defense contractor did a pilot ABC study of its materials-handling processes to better understand how to allocate those costs to various projects. It discovered that for every dollar it spent on materials, it spent another dollar on storing and handling those materials. This startling revelation led to a complete reengineering of the materials-handling process. As long as materials-handling costs were buried in the broad category of overhead, no one would ever have thought to look at the process itself.

Other Methods

The methodology a company uses is relatively unimportant. What is important is to involve a cross-functional team, or set of teams, in doing the analysis. The process of doing the charting and analysis is itself an educational process through which participants develop a thorough understanding of how the business works. Without such an understanding, effective improvements in business processes cannot happen.

In the mid-1970s, a plant manager at Caterpillar tried an experiment: He had video crews come into the manufacturing plant to tape an entire day's work. Cross-functional teams then analyzed the tapes to see what improvements could be made. The results: Over the next several months, they eliminated thousands of hours of work. According to Caterpillar's Jim Despain, the important thing is "to keep working the details." Despain also makes the important point that this type of analysis must include people from all levels and functions within the plant. "The best ideas came from the operators themselves."

The *education* of employees comes from the simulations and actual hands-on charting and analysis of business processes. The *training* component teaches employees how to do those tasks.

Changes in Organizational Design

Stovepipe organizations force employees to have functional myopia—their vision is, by structure, limited to the perimeter of their group's stovepipe. One key to most of today's hot transformation programs is the creation of cross-functional teams, the purpose of which is to break down the stovepipes, to allow better communications and decision making at all levels of the company.

> Northern Telecom, in examining how to improve cross-functional cooperation, concluded that one of the major barriers to such cooperation was the number of job descriptions that existed within the corporation. Because jobs were so narrowly defined, the people holding those jobs worked hard to protect their work from any interference from others. Several years ago, there were 330 separate job descriptions just on the shop floor! Today, that number is 70. According to NT vice president James Marchant, "The goal is one." His logic is simple—if there is only one job description, there can be no cross-functional rivalry. Everyone would be measured on the same basis: making a contribution to the company's success.

Hierarchical, functional organizations were developed in many industries through most of the twentieth century. Industrial history provides good reasons for the growth and success of these types of organizations. But as we approach the twenty-first century, world markets and competition call for new forms of organization. The old style has been proven, time and time again, to be incapable of meeting the rapidly changing demands of today's business environment.

> British Petroleum (BP) is today working hard to transform its organization to become more responsive and profitable. Its massive bureaucracy, which was developed over many

decades (up through the 1980s), resulted in a business structure that resembled an eleven-by-seventy matrix of responsibilities (eleven business streams times seventy countries in which BP did business). And the result of this massive hierarchy? One American BP executive said, "We spent more time dividing up the pie than trying to make it bigger."[5]

There is no one form of organization that will suit every company. Many possible forms exist, but no matter what the form, several trends in organizational design are apparent.

- Organizations are becoming flatter, with fewer levels separating the top officers of the company from the lowest levels.

- Work teams, whether within a single function or cross-functional, are becoming key organizational units. They are being given more and more responsibilities that used to belong to higher-level managers—from problem solving to hiring to making capital investments.

- Cross-functional, and even cross-company, cooperation is becoming a key to reducing time and financial barriers.

- Profit and loss responsibility is being driven to lower and lower levels of the organization.

These trends all mandate the elimination of functional myopia. Organizational barriers to cross-functional cooperation must be eliminated.

Administrative Policies and Procedures

Countless attempts at organizational transformation have failed because changes in administrative policies and procedures needed to support the new programs were not made. Often, policies and procedures continue to reinforce old behaviors rather than encourage new ones.

A primary example of this conflict is in the compensation of teams. If the organization's measurement and reward systems are based on individual achievement, and team members are competing with each other to get the largest possible share of a limited pot of money, teamwork principles will be subverted. According to Edward E. Lawler III, director of the Center for Effective Organizations at the University of Southern California: "At best this leads people to focus solely on their own behavior and not on improving work systems and processes. At worst, it encourages them to sabotage one another's performance by hoarding information, ignoring coworkers' requests or even making others look bad."[6] Companies that are trying to move to team-based work systems are increasingly introducing team-based, rather than individual-based, measurement and reward systems.[7]

But team-based compensation systems are only one—albeit an important one—aspect of administrative policies and procedures. In an era of time-based competition, many organizations' procurement policies and procedures are so burdensome that they can just about halt progress. For example, why must a manager, who has responsibility for a $10 million budget, get as many as a dozen signatures (which can take a week or more just for the paperwork to travel its full route) on a purchase order for a $500 piece of equipment?

In other cases, the organization becomes paralyzed because there are no policies to cover particular situations. Xerox vice president Richard Palermo calls it "Palermo's Law": "If a problem has been bothering your company and your customers for years and won't yield, that problem is the result of a cross-functional dispute, where nobody has total control of the whole process."[8]

Policies and procedures in most companies were developed over a long period of time to ensure consistency in the application of rules and to simplify work methods. The basic problem is that most companies' policies and procedures were developed during the growth of bureaucracy and continue to reflect that bureaucracy. If they are not changed, they will perpetuate the bureaucracy, no matter what else is done to change the organization and its work methods. One solution to this problem is to subject the company's administrative policies and procedures to the same type of scrutiny being given to engineering, manufacturing, and customer service methods.

> Blount Canada Ltd. holds a quarterly "Accountability Forum" to assess progress toward company goals. Originally started in the early 1980s to focus on statistical quality control, today the forum includes all quality-related initiatives, including JIT, SPC, Experimental Design, and other methods. The forum includes the division vice president and all production managers. According to Blount's Eugene Kraemer, the forum recently has been extended to staff and service groups, including human resources, accounting, and maintenance, recognizing that these groups also must be accountable for how their operations affect overall company results.

Some companies are taking the concept of "customer satisfaction" and extending it to include *internal* as well as external customers. Many companies, in both manufacturing and service industries, have in recent years tried to become much more "customer-focused." They have completely rewritten their customer-related policies and procedures to achieve the desired levels of responsiveness.

What would happen if each function within a company identified its internal customers and applied the same customer-satisfaction criteria to those audiences? The results can be extraordinary. For example, in one company, the mission of the company's legal department turned 180 degrees. The job of the legal department used to be to "keep the company out of trouble." To do this job, the company lawyers tried to identify every possible legal problem that could arise from a proposed company action, and then to create the legal documents that would ensure that no adverse action could possibly take place. The result was that many proposed company programs got so tied up in the legal department that they never saw the light of day—"too much risk," at least from the legal standpoint. After the transformation of the legal department's mission, its job was redefined to concentrate on: "How can we help the company get its job done?"

When one large corporation tried to hire me to do an on-site workshop, its purchasing department sent me all of their standard consultant agreements. These included giving the company ownership of any materials used in the seminar or workshop, providing evidence of a performance bond, signing of noncompetitive agreements, etc. It took a while for the hiring manager in the company to convince the purchasing and legal departments that I was being hired for the expertise I was bringing to the company, that I owned my instructional materials, which I had used with many other customers, and that this would be a one-shot deal—I would be at the company for two days and then be gone. Once all this was explained, the requirements changed. All that the legal department now wanted was for me to sign a standard nondisclosure agreement—this was not a barrier.

The difference here was that the legal department switched its view from assuming that the instructor was a potential threat to the company to one in which the instructor was a potential asset.

GETTING CUSTOMERS AND SUPPLIERS INTO FOCUS

All of the issues relating to functional myopia apply equally to a company's relationships with its customers and suppliers. More and more organizations are entering into partnerships with their customers and suppliers. In many cases, such relationships are multifaceted—two aerospace companies, for example, may simultaneously be partners involved with one group of projects, competitors in other arenas, customers of each other for specialized products or services, and at the same time have several lawsuits pending against each other. To say that these relationships are tricky is a gross understatement.

The same myopia that exists within functions inside a company is likely to be applied when dealing with the company's suppliers, with equally poor results.

> A major chemical company was having a problem with a raw ingredient supplied by a smaller company. While there was a range of purity allowed in each thousand-pound batch delivered, the contract required that each batch be consistent throughout, that is, a 95 percent pure batch had to be consistently 95 percent pure—half couldn't be 93 percent and the other half 97 percent. After a series of increasingly hostile letters and phone calls to the supplier, the company sent one of its engineers to visit the supplier's plant. The problem was that the supplier's manufacturing process only made eight hundred pounds at a time. The thousand-pound order required them to mix different batches together, resulting in inconsistent quality. The company engineer called his purchasing department—why did they order everything in thousand-pound batches? The reason: Purchasing had standardized on thousand-pound lot sizes to make its purchase orders simpler to handle. There was nothing in the company's manufacturing process that mandated the thousand-pound batch. The solution: Change the lot size to eight hundred pounds. The supplier was so relieved to hear this that he offered to lower the price.

As organizations examine their value chains to attempt to overcome their functional myopia, it is important that they include their entire value chain, both internal and external to the organization itself. The point of the exercise is to maximize the value added throughout the entire chain, for the company to maximize its overall productivity and profitability. When functions operate only to maximize their local goals, they lose sight of the larger picture and often make decisions that cannot be justified in the larger context.

KEY POINTS

The third foundation for the learning organization is "overcoming functional myopia"—getting people at all levels and across all functions to widen their focus from their local goals and standards to the overall goals of the organization. The three primary causes of functional myopia are cultural, organizational, and administrative barriers that have developed as the organization has grown over time. To eliminate functional myopia requires education and training programs, changes in organizational design to eliminate structural barriers, and rethinking administrative policies and procedures to ensure that they support overall company goals.

FIVE

BUILDING AND SUSTAINING EFFECTIVE "LEARNING" TEAMS

Whether within a single function or across functional, organizational, and company boundaries, effective teamwork enables people to learn from each other, to increase awareness of and access to information, and to find better ways of working that would otherwise not be possible. Effective teams have achieved seemingly unattainable results in many companies, results that would not have been possible without them.

> At Honeywell's Building Controls Division, Concurrent Engineering teams were used to replace the old, sequential approach to product development. The product development team started by "abandoning a three-inch-thick volume documenting product development procedures in favor of a twenty-page guideline." The result: "[The Product Development Cycle] was reduced from two to three years under the old methods to fourteen months."[1]

> At Hoechst Celanese Corporation's Salisbury, North Carolina, plant, multiskilled teams are enhancing performance and competitiveness. According to plant manager Carl Repsher, these teams "have reduced costs by at least $8 million annually through productivity improvements."[2]

But teamwork is not the standard way of working for most American organizations—most employees are more familiar with ideals of individual competition and achievement.

As a result, creating effective learning teams is not a trivial exercise. People carry a lot of baggage with them that must be overcome if they are to work effectively as part of a team. Organizations also throw up roadblocks to effective teamwork in the form of organizational, cultural, and administrative barriers.

Within the past few years, several dozen books have been written on the need for teamwork in American industry, and today there are literally hundreds of training vendors and consultants who actively market their own approaches to creating teams. Millions of dollars are being spent by organizations, large and small, to train teams. So why aren't results like those cited in the previous examples being reported everywhere?

Unfortunately, in many organizations, groups of people are simply assembled and told that they are now to work as a team. It is assumed that effective teamwork will immediately result. Some of these organizations may even provide a one- or two- or even five-day program on team skills, and then leave the team on its own to accomplish its goals. This doesn't work, for several reasons.

BARRIERS TO EFFECTIVE TEAMWORK

First, *many people don't believe in teamwork*. It is not uncommon for each member of a newly formed cross-functional team to get the same instructions from his or her manager. "They want us to work as part of this team. You and I both know that our approach to this problem [or project or program] is the right one. Your job is to go convince the rest of the team to do it our way."

Second, *measurement and reward systems often remain keyed to individual rather than team achievement.* This means that the self-interested employee will work toward demonstrating his or her superior achievement, even if it means reducing attainment of over-all team goals.

Third, *any new set of skills takes time to learn, practice, and master.* If these opportunities are not provided, individual team members quickly will revert to what has worked in the past—the individual skills that they have mastered over most of their careers.

Fourth, *many managers are loath to hand over their hard-won responsibilities and prerogatives to any team.* As one manager from an aerospace company told me, "I've worked hard to get where I am, and I make good decisions. I'm not about to voluntarily hand over my decision-making power to any team. If I give up that power, what do I have left?"

DEVELOPING EFFECTIVE LEARNING TEAMS

To become an effective, self-managed learning team requires a group of people to go through four stages of development, in each stage learning and practicing new skills. The result will be a team that not only manages its work, but also itself. These stages are:

1. Formation.
2. Development of team skills.
3. Development of management skills.
4. Self-management.

Table 5.1 lists the major development activities that take place in each of these four stages.

Table 5.1
Stages in Team Development

Stages in Team Development	Major Activities
Stage 1. Team formation	■ Establish membership. ■ Define roles and responsibilities. ■ Establish norms of behavior. ■ Determine schedules. ■ Establish reporting mechanisms.
Stage 2. Team skills development	■ Develop needed skills (communications, cooperative work, meeting management, negotiating, conflict resolution). ■ Pratice and reinforce skills as work is done by the team.
Stage 3. Management skills development	■ Develop needed management skills. ■ Migrate management responsibilities from team manager to team.
Stage 4. Self-management	■ Complete migration from team manager to team.

STAGE 1. FORMATION

When an organization decides to build a team for a specific purpose, whether it's to improve customer responsiveness, develop a new product, or implement JIT on the manufacturing floor, care must be exercised in planning how that team should be formed. *One* person (the team manager) must have the responsibility of creating the team and getting it started. This exercise includes:

- Determining what groups or functions need to be represented on the team.

- Getting buy-in on the team goals and concept from each function to be represented on the team.

- Identifying and recruiting candidates for team membership.

Any team starts out as a group of individuals. Its first work is to become a team. In selecting the members of the team, the team manager explains to each person the scope of the team's charter and responsibilities—why it is being formed and what it is expected to accomplish, as well as the role that the team manager expects the individual to play on the team. It is vital that all team members accept these definitions and their roles on the team. Without this basic understanding and agreement, little can be accomplished by the team.

A mid-level manager in the company's MIS division asked two of the company's top instructors to train a team of ten people whose job it was to serve internal customers. At the initial training session, the trainers asked a series of introductory questions: "How long have you been working as a team?" No response. "What are your team goals?" No response. Finally, "Do you consider yourselves a team?"

After several silent minutes, the answer came back: "No, we aren't a team."

"Then why are you here for team training?" asked the instructors.

"Because our manager told us to be here."

The instructors then did what I consider both the right thing to do and what I don't think most instructors would do—they sent the "team" back to its office and went to meet with the manager who had arranged the training. They explained to her that creating an effective team requires more than sending a bunch of people to a training session.

At an initial team meeting, the charter, roles, and responsibilities are explained to the full team. The first few meetings are spent developing a common understanding of these items. As they work together, the team members can get to know each other better. Norms of behavior (for example, team members may disagree with each other in team meetings, but team decisions must always be supported when dealing with people and groups outside the team) are established early on in the team meetings.

During the first few meetings, agreements are reached on how team members will work together on team tasks, and a schedule of activities and meetings is established. Responsibilities and milestones are agreed on and reporting mechanisms established. The role of the team manager with respect to team members is explicitly defined.

It should be noted here that this is *not*, at this stage, a self-managed, empowered work team. The goals of the team, its membership, and the basic rules are *given* to the team (see table 5.2). As the team progresses through subsequent stages of development, these responsibilities will migrate increasingly from the manager to the team itself.

STAGE 2. DEVELOPMENT OF TEAM SKILLS

Once the basic ground rules are established and agreed to, the team members must start to learn a new set of skills—team skills. These include:

- Communications skills.
- Cooperative work skills.
- Meeting management skills.
- Negotiating skills.
- Conflict resolution skills.

Table 5.2
Team Responsibilities: Stage 1 into Stage 2

Responsibility	Team Manager	Team Members
Team membership	Recruit team members Replaces members as needed	Show up
Team goals	Set by team manager	Accept
Team roles	Set by team manager	Accept
Team reporting	Reports sent to team manager Manager reports to outside world	Prepare reports for team manager
Team meetings	Run by team manager	Participate
Conflict resolution	Done by team manager	Report conflicts to team manager
Work toward goals	Defined by team manager	Done by team members
Interface with world outside team	Done by team manager	None

While most of these skills are also included in the foundation of "thinking" literacy, they merit repeating here.

Communications Skills

Communications skills are necessary to ensure that team members understand each other and can communicate their own ideas clearly. They enable open communications and sharing of ideas, and ensure that valuable ideas will not be lost just because they are poorly communicated.

Cooperative Work Skills

Cooperative work skills help the individual members of the team to better work together. Many new team members are so used to working alone that the idea of working with other people is foreign to them. Cooperative work skills begin with the development of an understanding of the overall work of the team and how each person's work fits into that overall pattern. This can be done by process modeling, by the concept of value chains (each person looks at his customers and suppliers in the chain from concept to finished product or service), or simply by spending time with other team members to find out what they are doing and how it relates to the other team members' work.

During a one-day Concurrent Engineering workshop given by former Xerox vice president Barry Bebb, he spent the day talking about the need for teamwork and about various Concurrent Engineering methodologies. At the end of the day, he took some questions from the audience. One person asked, "I am a senior engineer, heading up a small design group for a new product. I hear, and agree with all that you have said here today. But my manager doesn't believe in Concurrent Engineering. How can I get some of the benefits you are describing without getting my manager to buy into changing our whole approach?"

Bebb spent a couple of minutes thinking about the question and then responded, "Here's what you can do. Find out where your new product is going to be manufactured. Call the plant manager and tell him that you want to bring your team to the plant for a day. Suggest that your team and his staff share ideas about how you all can make your lives easier. Get the communications going—that's what it is all about. Most rational managers will support open cooperation."

All of the other skill areas listed here are necessary for the team to operate as a team. Cooperative work skills are what enables the team to get its job done—to achieve synergy in decreasing labor, time, cost, or defects, whatever the team's goals happen to be. Cooperative work requires that every member of the team be free of functional myopia and open to new ideas and ways of working. The way in which team members learn from each other is through cooperative work.

Meeting Management Skills

Since much of the work of teams is done in meetings, the acquisition of meeting management skills will be a great asset to the entire team, helping them avoid the common meeting syndrome in which "minutes are taken and hours are wasted." There are many meeting management manuals and workshops available in the market. While no one method of meeting management stands out as being vastly superior to others, one technique should be chosen and training provided, either by the team manager or by an internal or external facilitator.

As with all new skills, a one-shot training effort is generally *not* sufficient to ensure the consistent, ongoing application of the training. Coaching and reinforcement by the team manager, the training facilitator, or another skilled facilitator should continue through at least several meetings to ensure that the team has mastered the new skills.

Negotiating Skills

Negotiating skills are necessary to resolve differences that will inevitably arise. When a group of individual contributors starts working as a team, members must learn to view their goals in light of the overall work of the team, rather than from their functional perspectives alone. This requires trade-offs between competing objectives and standards, and these trade-offs cannot always be made through the evaluation of strictly technical criteria. For example, improving customer satisfaction within a telephone service center may demand that operators be allowed more time per call, or decreasing manufacturing cost may require that the corners on a piece of equipment be square, rather than round, even though this may be a "less elegant" design. These types of trade-offs must be negotiated within the team.

Conflict Resolution Skills

When any group of people works together for the first time, some level of conflict will almost always occur. Conflicts may occur on a personal level or because the goals and standards of the various functions represented on the team are sometimes at odds with each other. Whatever the cause, the team will face internal conflicts and, therefore, should be prepared to resolve these problems.

Shifting Roles and Responsibilities

As each new set of skills is learned and mastered, the team will assume more and more of the responsibilities for managing its own work, reducing the role of the team manager. By the end of Stage 2, the team should be planning its own work, running its own meetings, resolving its own internal conflicts, and managing its own reporting systems (see table 5.3). The team manager's role at this point is reduced to the administrative management of the team (determining membership, replacing members who may leave the team, evaluating individual and team performance, etc.) and providing the interface with the outside world.

Table 5.3
Team Responsibilities: End of Stage 2

Responsibility	Team Manager	Team Members
Team membership	Recruit team members Replaces members as needed	Show up
Team goals	Set by team manager	Input
Team roles	Input	Set by team
Team reporting	Reports sent to team manager Manager reports to outside world	Set up reporting mechanisms Prepare reports for team manager
Team meetings	Participate	Run meetings
Conflict resolution	Handle conflicts with outside world	Resolve own conflicts within team
Work toward goals	Input	Defined and done by team members
Interface with world outside team	Done by team manager	None

Bill Picott, a senior engineering manager at Digital Equipment Corporation, describes the team manager's role in this way: "In the sport of curling, players push a heavy stone down the ice, with the "skip" [the captain of the curling team] skating in front of the disk, sweeping its path, to make certain that nothing gets in its way. The team manager's job is that of the sweeper—clearing obstacles so that the players [team members] can focus on their work."

Even as the team starts assuming more responsibility for its own management, the team manager remains involved as coach and adviser throughout Stage 2. No new set of skills is ever immediately flawless in its application. The job of the team manager throughout Stage 2 is to monitor the team's learning and work methods and to provide coaching and additional instruction when needed.

STAGE 3. DEVELOPMENT OF MANAGEMENT SKILLS

By the beginning of Stage 3, the team is running its own meetings, setting its own work procedures, and generally taking care of all internal workings. The team manager's role, at this point, is to provide the interface with the world outside the team. He has insulated the team from outside negotiations and conflicts and has handled administrative matters such as team measurements and rewards.

As the team learns, it slowly assumes the management tasks still being done by the team manager. For example, up to this point, if a team member left the team, the team manager was responsible for recruiting a replacement. As team management skills increase, the team itself will take greater responsibility for its own membership, setting its own goals, and interfacing with the external organization of which it is a part.

During this stage, team members must learn a new set of skills—management skills. These include:

- Personnel management, including how to measure and reward team members' job performance.

- Conflict resolution, including dealing with the larger organization of which the team is a part.

- Goal setting, including how to set/negotiate the team's goals within the larger organization.

While these topics may be the subject of formal training programs, it is more likely that the team manager will provide the needed instruction on an ad hoc basis, getting the team more and more involved in the administrative tasks as time progresses. Instead of representing the team to higher-level management himself, the team manager will start bringing team members to meetings and eventually will let the team members make the presentations and do the negotiations, acting only as adviser and coach. The same pattern will repeat itself with salary planning, budgeting for the next period, and so forth. Gradually, all administrative responsibilities will migrate from the team manager to the team itself. At the end of Stage 3, the team manager's role will disappear, leaving a fully empowered, self-managed team.

STAGE 4. SELF-MANAGEMENT

At Stage 4, the fully empowered, self-managed team has emerged, ready to tackle the goals of TQM, the learning organization, or any other major business initiative. At this point, there is no team manager—the team is managing itself. However, it is important that the relationship between the team and the former team manager not be entirely severed.

The former team manager is a person who has had a lot of experience in the organization, probably more than any of the team members. He knows the team members well and knows what challenges they will probably face as they progress in their work. Even though he has moved on to other responsibilities in the company, the former team manager should maintain contact with the team and should be available as a coach and mentor.

HOW LONG SHOULD IT TAKE?

How long it takes a team to go through all four stages of development will depend on a number of factors:

- The skill of the team manager in forming the team.

- The quality and timing of training provided to the team.

- The nature of the team's work.

- The abilities of team members to learn new work methods.

The Skill of the Team Manager

The initial negotiations between the team manager and the functions to be represented on the team are vital to team success. These negotiations include setting of basic guidelines for team operation, reaching agreement on team goals, and selection of team members. All team members must be empowered to represent their respective functions. If this does not happen, and team decisions are rejected routinely or altered by a team member's functional manager, not only will time be lost, but that member will lose all credibility with the rest of the team as well.

In one electronics company, a cross-functional team was appointed to design a new product. Joe, the team's design engineer, was pushing for his initial design. Fred, the team's representative from manufacturing engineering, told Joe that the design should be altered to reduce manufacturing costs. Rather than negotiate the solution within the team, Joe went over Fred's head to the manager of manufacturing engineering. He then came back to the team and reported: "Well, I talked with Fred's manager last week. He not only liked my design, but said that his folks had solved tougher problems than this one in the past."

The point here was not that Joe's design wasn't manufacturable, but that it was too costly to manufacture. Joe's move destroyed Fred's credibility on the team and made it impossible for the team to continue working together. The fault for this problem lies both with Joe, who violated team norms by going over Fred's head, and with Fred's manager who disempowered his representative on the team.

The team manager's effectiveness in reaching necessary agreements up front and in selecting team members who will play by the rules will dictate the speed at which the team will be able to move through the first and subsequent stages of development.

Quality and Timing of Training

Team training can be provided by the team manager (if that person has the necessary skills), by an internal training group, or an external trainer. The source of the training is less important than the skill of the instructor, the timing of the training, and the follow-up and reinforcement provided. The ideal is to provide "Just-in-Time" (JIT) training, or what some call "demand-pull" training.

Under these concepts, training is provided when it is needed or demanded, rather than according to a predetermined schedule. If a team finds itself at an impasse because of conflicting goals among the various members, they may ask for training on negotiations techniques. If there are problems keeping track of all project-related activities, the team may ask for project management training. When training is provided on an as-needed basis, team members see its relevance and thereby can immediately apply the information they receive. The result is that the training itself becomes more valuable because it is being immediately used to help meet team, and therefore company, business objectives.

Some companies have put together a small group of team trainers/facilitators to provide JIT team training. They provide some start-up training and then attend team meetings on a periodic basis. When they see a problem arise, they reach into their toolkit and pull out a module of instruction and provide the needed instruction on the spot. In other cases, they may provide reminders and reinforcement for training already received.

Too often, training is heavily front-loaded. That is, a multiday course is given to newly formed teams with the assumption that they will learn everything they need in one intensive session. This is not a good solution, for several reasons:

- Team members are likely to suffer from information overload.

- Not yet having worked as a team, members may not recognize the need for various topics being presented. Without this perceived need, learning will not be as effective.

- The right time to provide training on any topic is just as it is needed. With JIT training, trainees then see the immediate relevance of the material, welcome the training, and start to implement it at once.

Dan Sirmans, senior consulting manager for organization development and training at Carrier Corporation, in describing his approach to team development, uses the analogy of a railroad engine. "If you look at a railroad locomotive, you'll see that the wheels on either side don't move simultaneously—they work in lockstep fashion." So it is with technical and team development at Carrier. Ralph Bott, an internal OD consultant working with Carrier's Transicold Division, uses a sociotechnical approach, which coordinates technical training and social skills training and development so they move in this lockstep fashion. Team development activities are carried out at the rate of three hours per week over a four-month period. A similar schedule is used with technical training on Carrier's "Lean Production System." Leadership development activities parallel the other areas, with team coaches receiving four and one-half hours of training per week. The results thus far, two years into the program, are that Transicold has reached the highest production levels in its history.

The Nature of the Team's Work

There are many types of teams put in place for many different purposes. The complexity of the team's work has a major effect on how fast the team can move through the four stages of development. If, for example, team working methods are well established and require minimal cross-training, movement through Stage 2 will occur much faster than if the team has difficulty establishing new functional work methods as well as new cross-functional work techniques.

> At Northern Telecom's Bramalea plant in Brampton, Ontario, the "Circuit Pack Area Team" has responsibility for the assembly of circuit packs into empty frames and a number of associated activities. The team has responsibility for meeting production quotas, interfacing with other departments and groups as necessary, and managing their own work schedules.
>
> Because its tasks are closely related, and work methods well defined, this team is very effective in cross-training members on the various activities, helping each other out in peak work times, and filling in for each other when the need arises.
>
> Digital Equipment Corporation's storage systems group, in developing its RA90 disk drive in the mid-1980s, formed a product development team that had a very different set of challenges from those of Northern Telecom's Circuit Pack

Area Team. In trying to leapfrog the competition, the team was developing both a new product and new manufacturing technologies simultaneously. Because neither the engineering nor the manufacturing work methods for these new technologies were well defined, the team had to spend much more time developing both functional and cross-functional work methods.

The work methods for the Northern Telecom team were much better defined than those for the Digital team, so its journey through Stage 2 happened much more quickly.

Team Members' Skill Levels

The abilities of team members, in terms of both their functional skills and their team skills, will have direct impact on team effectiveness. In any organization, there is not an equal distribution of functional skills among all employees in a department. The company may have three or thirty or three hundred engineers, but they will not be equally skilled. It is vital that the team manager do a good job of defining up front the skills needed on the team as well as negotiating with functional management to ensure that each functional representative on the team has the requisite skills. The team manager's success in obtaining the right personnel for the team will depend on:

- How important the team project is to each functional manager.

- Competing demands from other projects or work that require the same set of skills as those being sought for the team project.

If team members do not bring team skills with them, it is equally important that they at least arrive with willingness to work as part of the team and a desire to learn team skills. The fact is that not all employees want to work on a team. There are many people who prefer working in isolation, carving out their little piece of the world and working solely on that piece.

It is incumbent on the team manager (and, later on, on the team as a whole) to identify skill deficiencies in either area and to remedy those deficiencies either by arranging for needed training or by replacing team members who cannot get the job done. Allowing a poor performer to continue with a team not only reduces the overall efficiency of the team, but also destroys team cohesiveness and morale. As Ramiro Mendoza, a group leader at Subaru-Isuzu Automotive, Inc., points out: "A team is similar to a battery, you know. If you let one cell go dead, then it's much harder to get the car started."[3]

How Long Should It Take?

There are no time norms for team development, because every team is different. In some companies, effective, self-managed work teams have been developed in as little as two years. In others, it has taken much longer. RoseAnn Stevenson, manager of organizational and management development for the Boeing Company, says, "Many companies who want to install this [team] process think they can do it in a year or two. I'd say four to five years is more realistic."[4] No matter how long the entire journey takes, effective teamwork can begin much more quickly, starting in Stage 2, *if* you have effective team managers and provide effective team training.

AD HOC TEAMS

There will be times when a company needs to appoint a temporary, ad hoc team, to handle a specific problem or task over a specified period of time (usually less than six months). When the task is completed, the team will be dissolved. In these circumstances, there will not be sufficient time to go through the team development process. Therefore, the company must ensure that either (a) all people appointed to the team already have proven team skills, or (b) that the team has a strong team manager who can guide the team through its work.

DISTRIBUTED TEAMS

In many larger companies, members of a single team may come from many different sites, even from different countries. While the principles and practices of team development described in this chapter apply equally to these distributed teams, there are several differences between distributed teams and single-site teams:

- To foster team cohesiveness, it is important that the entire team be co-located for an initial period of time (ranging from several weeks to several months). Team members need to get to know each other as people in order to build the trust necessary for effective team-work. Relationships developed during this start-up phase may be continued long-distance, but it helps everyone involved to be able to associate a telephone voice or fax or E-mail message with a real person.

- Distributed teams will, of necessity, use a variety of telephone- and computer-based technologies to maintain communications among team members. Regular communication becomes even more important for a distributed team—it is the only way that far-flung team members can be reminded constantly that they are indeed working as part of a team.

■ Computer-based "groupware" tools for project planning and reporting become even more important for a distributed team, ensuring that everyone on the team has constant access to all necessary project-related information.

INTERCOMPANY TEAMS

Another strong trend today is the formation of teams within networks of companies.[5] Again, the stages of development for a multicompany team are the same as for a single-company team. Intercompany teams, however, raise even greater levels of concern about trust among team members—it is common today for two companies to be cooperating on one project while competing on others.

Although companies that are striving to become learning organizations typically start within, there are many benefits to be gained by harnessing the information and knowledge of their customers and suppliers by building effective intercompany teamwork.

> Eric Middelstadt, CEO of GMFanuc Robotics, describes what can happen when a supplier is not brought into the planning cycle early on: "We could have saved a customer thousands of dollars just by explaining where to put a hole in the trunk of a car. The hole was needed to complete the paint job, but the company didn't put the hole in the right place, and we didn't get involved early enough. The result: We had to put a fixture on the trunk lid to open it up. . . . The customer had to pay a lot of money for all the fixtures. Paint got on the fixtures, flaked off and messed up the paint job. . . . If the customer had involved us a couple of months earlier, we would have foreseen the problem and advised him accordingly."[6]

KEY POINTS

To achieve effective teamwork, companies must overcome a set of personal, cultural, and structural barriers. This requires a four-stage development process, starting with team formation and continuing through the acquisition of team skills and management skills by team members. The role of team manager is vital in the formation and development of teams. The four-stage model results in effective, self-managed learning teams and a variety of associated benefits, including reductions in cost, time, and defects.

As team managers guide teams through the four-stage process, their team-related job responsibilities lessen. The team manager role will be new to most companies. Team managers generally will come from the ranks of middle managers—a new role for managers, as will be discussed in the next chapter.

SIX

MANAGERS AS ENABLERS

The role of management has changed greatly since the heyday of the large, hierarchical corporation. Companies by the thousands are compressing their pyramids, decimating the ranks of middle management. Where middle managers had traditionally been a primary conduit of company information, new information technologies have made many of their jobs unnecessary. Similarly, the movement to self-managed work teams has eliminated the need for many middle managers.

> Caterpillar's Transmissions Business Unit started out as an old-style hierarchy, with five levels from the business unit general manager to the worker on the factory floor. Today, there are two levels: the managing Business Council and a group of nineteen self-managed work teams. Fourteen of the work teams are classified as "revenue-producing" while five are "service units." Each work team includes former first-line and middle managers along with factory floor workers.

The learning organization, TQM, Business Process Reengineering—any and all of today's hot transformation initiatives—call for management to assume new roles with respect to their subordinates. They require the creation of empowered, *self-managed* work teams. The result is fewer traditional middle management jobs, with very different sets of responsibilities and accountabilities for those that remain. Whether they stay in a newly defined middle management role or take a different role, today's middle managers, along with their accumulated knowledge of the company's business, values, and experience, can be invaluable resources in helping their companies to become learning organizations.

THE CHANGING ROLE OF MIDDLE MANAGERS

"Many observers say this is the end of middle management. They're right. Nothing will ever be the same for middle managers again."[1]
—Thomas R. Horton, CEO
American Management Association

Not only are organizations becoming flatter, meaning that thousands of management jobs are being eliminated, but the jobs of the remaining managers are being redefined, as outlined in table 6.1.

While these new management roles become more widespread each day, changing long-practiced behaviors is not easy. The new directions are clear, but many middle managers struggle with the mixed messages they receive from their own management.

- Take risks, but don't fail.

- Build long-term capabilities, but ensure short-term results.

- Build empowered work teams, but make certain that nothing goes wrong.

Table 6.1
**Traditional and
Modern Management Styles***

Traditional Style	Modern Style
Strict manager-employee relationship	More function and peer relationships
Give orders	Negotiate
Carry messages up and down	Solve problems and make decisions
Job description and prescribed specific tasks	Create your own, entrepreneurial job role
Narrow, functional focus	Broad, cross-functional collaboration
Go through channels sequentially	Attain speed and flexibility
Control employees	Coach employees

* Adapted from Thomas R. Horton and Peter C. Reid, *Beyond the Trust Gap* (Homewood, IL: Business One Irwin, 1991).

■ Train your people, but be sure that current productivity isn't compromised.

These mixed signals reflect both the pressure being felt by senior managers and their own unease at making changes in their own behavior. To succeed, senior managers need the lessons of leadership (the first foundation), including commitment and constancy. Middle managers who are required to move to new models of management need both training and reinforcement to ensure that the required new skills are both learned and practiced.

Transforming the Middle Manager

To succeed with the new model, middle managers first need to learn new skills. These new skills and management practices, as presented in table 6.1, are very different from those they have both experienced and practiced in the past. The most effective trainers of middle managers will be senior management, because this will make the messages immediately clear, relevant, and important.

> Brian Jones, president of NYPRO's Clinton plant, not only teaches the managers who report to him, but also requires them to spend at least 5 percent of their time training their people, through formal classes or through one-on-one coaching. Topics range from team building to the company's safety program. Jones feels that this practice gives employees the right message—they are important enough to merit direct attention and instruction from their managers. It also makes it immediately clear that they are expected to implement what they are being taught.

If senior managers feel that they do not have the skills to provide the instruction themselves, formal instruction may be given by internal or external trainers. In these cases, senior management cannot just bow out—they must attend the training sessions themselves. This demonstrates their commitment to the new model and stresses its importance. It also enables them to provide ongoing reinforcement and coaching as their middle managers start applying the new approach.

Preparing for
the New Middle Management Role

Middle managers must learn a new set of skills to succeed under the new model. When they were merely a conduit between higher and lower levels of the organization, they needed a set of administrative skills. Now, they are expected to run their own businesses, often being given profit and loss responsibility in place of functionally specialized work. Under the old model, they pushed problems up the hierarchy and implemented the decisions downward. Now, they are required to analyze their own problems and implement their own decisions. The functional bureaucracy within which they operated is now being replaced with cross-functional relationships and teamwork. All of these changes require retraining in two major areas:

- Understanding and running a business.
- Building, maintaining, and coaching a team.

Middle managers increasingly are being required to run their operations as an independent business, with profit and loss responsibility. Even if they remain a service unit or cost center, they now face both internal and external competition for their groups' work—if cost, time, and quality requirements cannot be met internally, their companies will outsource their work and disband their groups. To survive in this new business environment, middle managers must acquire new business skills. They must understand how their work fits into the company's overall business, how to work with the rest of the company (rather than within a single function), and how to build their own business. Their role is being transformed from functional manager to general business manager, requiring a full set of business management skills.

Just as the middle manager must change the way he relates to the business, so he must also learn new practices with regard to his employees. He must become teacher, team builder, and coach. All of these new roles require training and ongoing coaching, from senior management or from internal or external trainers.

Not everyone currently in a middle management job is cut out for the new role of "manager as enabler." Often, in creating new middle management roles, companies (such as Tellabs and British Telecom) make incumbents reapply for the new jobs. This allows the company to select those candidates who are most suited to the new positions. Unfortunately, in most of these cases, the number of incumbents greatly exceeds the number of new jobs, displacing large numbers of middle managers.

ALTERNATIVE ROLES
FOR DISPLACED MIDDLE MANAGERS

In stripping out levels of middle management, companies often discard large groups of employees whose knowledge and experience cannot be replaced. These "expendable" middle managers often have:

- A decade or more of experience in the company.

- Outstanding achievement records (or they would not have been promoted to middle management).

- Intimate knowledge of the company, its products, its customers, and suppliers.

- More knowledge than most others in the company about how things work and how work gets done.

- Substantial insights about how the company's business can be improved.

These middle managers are, therefore, among the most valuable *knowledge assets* within the company. So while the company may no longer need as many middle managers, it can be harmed by tossing these assets aside (or swiftly out the door). Knowledge assets cannot be replaced easily.

Alternative roles for at least some portion of these middle managers can maximize the company's return on these valuable assets, and on the large investments the company has already made in these people. The transition to new roles will not come easily to middle managers. They will need to deal with their own perceived loss of rank, status, and privilege, at the same time refocusing on a whole new career path.

> In one company, a group of middle managers were assembled and told that their jobs were changing. While none of them was being fired, they would be given other roles and responsibilities as individual contributors in various functional areas. One manager asked, "What am I supposed to tell my family?" with a noticeable choke in his voice.
>
> In a later one-on-one meeting with a senior company manager, he explained, "I'm one of ten children, and the first to get off the farm and go to college. My family has followed my career in this company with great pride, celebrating each promotion, each step up the ladder. Now, I'm no longer on the ladder. What am I going to tell my parents, my brothers, my wife, my children?"

Even while defining new roles for former middle managers, companies need to pay attention to the psychological effects these changes have on their employees. There are many possible alternative roles for these former middle managers. Our focus will be on four specific roles:

- Teacher.
- Team manager.
- Intrapreneur.
- Strategic relations manager.

From Middle Manager to Teacher

To succeed in becoming a learning organization, implementing TQM or Business Process Reengineering, almost everyone in the corporation will need to learn one or more new sets of skills. Middle managers, by virtue of years of company experience, often make very effective teachers. Even if they need to learn the subject matter before being able to teach it, they can immediately make it relevant to the company's culture and business issues, and to the concerns of the many employees who, like themselves, are struggling to understand how they fit into the new model.

The transition from middle manager to teacher requires helping the middle manager learn both the subject matter to be taught and basic instructional skills. But this a relatively small investment as compared with the company's other choice: trying to furnish an external instructor with the knowledge of the company's culture that is already second nature to the middle manager through his years of experience.

> Most of the staff of the Caterpillar Training Institute have worked in the company for as many as twenty or more years. Some had started out as factory apprentices and had risen to high-level plant management positions before joining the institute staff. Many feel that their new roles as teachers and facilitators give them a wider sphere of influence over the company's future than their former management jobs. And because of their extensive experience in the company, they have instant credibility with their audiences.

Not every middle manager can become an effective teacher. Teaching, whether in the public schools or in industry, has never had the status of other professional occupations. Some managers will disdain the opportunity as not being a suitable replacement for their former roles. Other managers will lack the basic communications skills necessary to become an effective teacher. And others will opt for other roles being described here, or will leave the company for employment elsewhere. For those few who do choose this new role, the benefits to themselves, their students, and the company as a whole can be outstanding.

From Middle Manager to Team Manager

As companies move to create self-managed work teams, they need to move these teams through the four stages of team development:

1. Formation.
2. Development of team skills.
3. Development of management skills.
4. Self-management.

This method of team development requires that each team begin its existence with a team manager. The team manager role starts out as a full-time responsibility, gradually requiring less and less of the manager's time as the team assumes various responsibilities for its own work and management.

The initial job of team manager includes:

- Building consensus from all groups to be represented on the team on the definition of the team's goals and responsibilities.

- Identifying the best resource from each group to be represented on the team and recruiting those resources.

- Getting agreement from each of the groups that the team member representing each group is empowered to speak for, and make commitments for, the group.

- Organizing the initial team meeting.

- Providing, or arranging for, initial team training.

- Managing team meetings.

- Insulating the team from external events unrelated to the team's work.

- Resolving conflicts within the team and between the team and external groups.

As the team begins acquiring teamwork skills, the team manager becomes an instructor concentrating on team-related skills. As these skills are developed, the time requirement for the team manager decreases as the team assumes more responsibility for its own work. Starting at 80 percent of the team manager's time, the requirements lessen to 40 percent as the team masters teamwork skills and moves on to acquisition of management skills (Stage 3).

In Stage 3, the team manager focuses on management skills, helping the team members take increasing responsibility for its own management and for interfacing with the rest of the company. Again, as the team learns its new roles and the associated skills, the team manager's time requirements decline from 40 percent at the start of this stage, to 5 percent at its completion.

Once the team becomes an empowered, self-managed work team, it may seem there is no role for the team manager at all. But no new operation works completely smoothly, and this model calls for the team manager to maintain an arm's-length relationship with the team as a resource person to help them over the eventual bumps in the road.

> Becoming a team manager requires a major change from the old middle manager mindset. At medical equipment maker Becton-Dickinson, the creation of teams was stymied by middle managers who weren't willing to cede control to the teams. According to vice president Jim Wessel, "We had to get over the mindset that said, 'I'm not in control, so it must be out of control.' "[2]

Former middle managers require training to become effective team managers. The team manager role requires a set of skills quite different from those possessed by the typical middle manager, including:

■ Negotiations skills—the team manager will actively negotiate the team's role within the large company as well as the individual roles within the team.

- Teaching and coaching skills—the team manager's major role in Stages 2 and 3 is teaching team-related and managerial skills to team members and then moving from the teaching role into a coaching role.

- Career and life planning skills—the former middle manager, in taking on the team manager role, is dramatically altering his career path. Similarly, the old career paths through the ranks of management are greatly diminished for team members. The team manager must master these skills to guide his own career and those of his team's members.

The team manager does not need to become a master teacher in all subjects that the team must study. There should be other resources available to provide key aspects of the training, either through the company's training department or from an external vendor. The availability of training resources will depend on how many teams the company is forming, on the overall company demand for such instruction. The skills acquired by the team manager will be of use not only in this one team assignment, but also in broadening the team manager's career options as his team-related job duties diminish over time.

There are no norms that stipulate how fast a team should pass through the various stages. Time requirements, as discussed in the chapter on effective teamwork, will vary with the skills of the team manager and the learning capabilities of the team members. Rough approximations, for the purpose of planning the team manager's responsibilities, are:

- Stage 1—one to three months.

- Stage 2—six to twelve months.

- Stage 3—six to twelve months.

- Stage 4—ongoing.

As the time requirements for the team manager lessen, she will have more time available for other responsibilities within the company. Depending on the company's needs, the team manager will have several options:

- To lead another emerging team.

- To move into one of the other new roles for middle managers described in this chapter.

- To move into a newly defined middle manager's role.

- To join another team as a team *member*.

From Middle Manager to Intrapreneur

The "intrapreneur" is a hero of American business. He is the person who comes up with an idea for a new product or service, usually related to the company's primary business, which brings new opportunities for profit and market share to the company.

Surveys of middle managers in American industry have shown that they have many ideas for improving aspects of their companies' business and for new opportunities for their companies. The old, hierarchical structure of many companies did not provide any avenue for these ideas to surface. In the transformed corporation, these ideas will easily make their way into the discussion arena.

Most companies that are downsizing provide their "excess" middle managers with some type of compensation package based on length of service and other formulas. Given that many middle managers have been employed by their companies for one or more decades, these packages typically provide at least several months of wages and benefits. But rather than handing middle managers their severance packages as they are escorted out the door, companies should give managers an opportunity to develop some of their intrapreneurial ideas, using a five-step plan for this process:

Step 1. Identify a group of middle managers who are in the "downsizing pool."

Step 2. As an alternative to the severance package they would normally be offered, give them the opportunity to develop one of their own ideas for a new business. Give them a fixed period of time in which to develop their idea into a business proposal. The time period should not exceed the number of weeks of severance pay they are being offered.

Step 3. Provide them with an intensive course on developing a business plan.

Step 4. Let them continue using their offices and support services as they develop the plan.

Step 5. At the end of the time period, they present their proposed business plan to a committee composed of top company managers. If the proposal is accepted, they stay with the company and lead the new business effort. If the proposal is not accepted, they leave the company with whatever they have remaining of their severance packages.

The AT&T Network Systems Group has institutionalized intrapreneurship through the creation of a New Opportunities Program. Seminars are regularly given on entrepreneurship, marketing, and other topics to interested employees. Employees develop proposals that are evaluated by an Opportunity Review Board. If an idea is accepted, the proposing employee is expected to become the program's "champion," that is, to take responsibility for implementing the proposal. Ideas do not always have to be proposals for new, groundbreaking businesses. According to AT&T's Don Trotter, "Many of the suggestions have been simple, but highly profitable, applications of existing services, such as offering grounding services to cable television companies."[3]

While AT&T's plan is not targeted specifically at helping to find new roles for obsolete middle managers, the principles involved remain the same. This type of plan costs a company very little, but may result in great gains from new business ideas. What the company is doing is maximizing the possible return on its investment in these knowledge assets, rather than abandoning them. From the employee's perspective, those who choose to take this option will feel more valued than if they had simply been dismissed from the company, and if the company decides not to opt for the proposal, the employee has a business idea ready to take elsewhere—to another company or to start his or her own business.

Not every middle manager in the "downsizing pool" will take this option. But this program can be very empowering for those who buy in, and may be very profitable for the company with little risk or extra expense being assumed.

From Middle Manager to Strategic Relations Manager

Few companies today are totally vertically integrated—totally self-reliant for everything from raw material production to after-sales service. Today's business world is one of interdependence, with value chains encompassing many suppliers and customers who may be scattered around the world. As companies strive to transform themselves, they also must pay attention to the external segments of their value chains, forming strategic relationships with key suppliers and customers. These strategic relationships can take many different forms, such as:

- Certifying key suppliers according to the company's new quality standards.

- Working with both suppliers and customers to facilitate both incoming and outgoing JIT deliveries.

- Forming basic research partnerships with other companies or universities, focused on new materials or manufacturing methods.

- Developing new sales channels in foreign markets.

- Developing joint ventures to enter new markets.

These and many other types of strategic initiatives, which are increasingly vital in forging a company's future, have often gone wanting for lack of interest or manpower. Why not focus some of the energies and capabilities of former middle managers on forging these and other types of strategic relationships?

As manufacturing capabilities increased from year to year, Digital Equipment Corporation had an excess of experienced plant managers and other high-level manufacturing personnel, most with twenty or more years of experience in the company. Rather than outplacing these knowledgeable resources, Digital created a new role, called the "manufacturing corporate account manager" (MCAM). Assigned to key manufacturing customers, the MCAM had a dual responsibility. First, he worked with the sales account manager to develop an understanding of the customer's manufacturing operations and also how Digital's manufacturing solutions could be sold to the customer. Given broad experience in Digital's manufacturing operations, the MCAM could walk into a customer plant and immediately relate on a personal level to the customer's manufacturing staff. The other half of the MCAM role was to identify manufacturing practices, from the same customers, that had potential for improving Digital's own manufacturing operations. This type of informal benchmarking was responsible not only for bringing new ideas in-house, but also for forging strategic relationships with key customers.

There are many key strategic roles that former middle managers might play that will enable a company to continue obtaining a return on their investment in these people. For example:

■ Many large companies, such as Honda of America, Caterpillar, and others have found it necessary and desirable to provide quality-related training and consultation to their suppliers—especially small suppliers who do not have their own training staffs.

■ Many companies have formed industry consortia to fund research and development activities that they themselves cannot afford to do alone. Examples include the Great Lakes Composites Consortium and Europe's Airbus Consortium. Even such traditional rivals as Chrysler, Ford, and General Motors have formed consortia such as the U.S. Advanced Battery Consortium to develop new batteries for future electric cars.

■ Other companies have formed university-based consortia, such as MIT's Leaders for Manufacturing Program, to fund research into future management, information technology, engineering, or manufacturing technologies and practices.

■ Competitors sometimes find it necessary or desirable to collaborate on large strategic programs, such as U.S. Department of Defense weapons programs or the Apple-IBM partnership for personal computer chip development.

There is virtually no company that cannot benefit from such partnerships and collaborations. These types of programs are extensions of the learning organization, in which companies are harnessing the knowledge of people outside, as well as inside, their own organizations.

CAN ALL MIDDLE MANAGERS BE SAVED?

As companies look at their flattening pyramids, thousands of middle managers are being caught in the crush. The fact is that many of today's middle managers are so stuck in their ways that they won't be able to change, to adapt to new work methods, new relationships, and the new types of roles being described here. In these cases, dismissal is probably the only alternative that companies have. The flattening of organizations is long overdue, and it is doubtful that even combining all of the new roles in any one company will provide enough new opportunities to save all former middle managers.

But even if these new roles create opportunities for only 10 to 25 percent of the displaced managers, the company will be accomplishing a number of important goals:

- ■ It will preserve its investment in these long-term employees. If these investments are merely discarded, there is no hope of gaining any return on them.

- ■ It will be utilizing these valuable resources to build the company's future, through exploring new strategic business opportunities, new markets, and new relationships. It is also demonstrating to its employees and stockholders that it is open to new ideas.

- ■ It will be sending a clear and important message to all of its employees and stockholders that it is concerned not only with cutting current costs but in creating a real, exciting, and profitable future as well.

- It will be investing in making the company a true learning organization.

> When top executives at Bethlehem Steel's Burns Harbor plant started finding new roles for many middle managers, often in different parts of the organization, they found an unexpected benefit: "the flowering of some managers who found their niche after switching to a new department. They showed surprising progress in new roles better suited to their skills and personalities."[4]

The fact is that many people currently in middle management roles in American companies arrived there through the "Peter Principle."[5] Having risen to their "level of incompetency," as author Laurence J. Peters puts it, they become stuck in a management role, even if they had been happier and more effective in a role as an individual contributor. The shake-up of middle management ranks presents new opportunities for many of those "stuck" at this level to find better, more suitable, and more fulfilling roles in their current companies or elsewhere.

KEY POINTS

In company after company, large numbers of middle managers are being terminated, and organizations are losing valuable knowledge assets that cannot easily be replaced.

What is needed is the redefinition of roles for middle managers, from "manager as controller" to "manager as enabler"—the fifth and final foundation for the learning organization. For those who remain in the middle of the hierarchy, a new set of skills will be required. For those who fall from the middle management ranks, there is a set of alternative roles that at least some can play to help their companies succeed in transforming themselves into learning organizations. While not all current middle managers will find new roles in the transformed organization, it behooves companies to hold on to their vital knowledge assets. You can't achieve any return on assets that you have abandoned.

SEVEN

INVESTING IN PEOPLE

"Management is beginning to realize that it is the combined knowledge of all of its employees that will differentiate them from their competition and will give them the competitive edge they need in the marketplace. . . . When companies begin to manage knowledge as an asset, a whole new set of disciplines will emerge. The new approach will influence the way executives think about economics, technology, human resources, and planning."
—Curtiss Frederick, President, Flexstar[1]

To become a learning organization, a company must *invest* in its people, for it is people who develop and use knowledge to meet company goals. The investment should start with building the foundations for the learning organization, from developing leaders to overcoming functional myopia to transforming managers into enablers.

Investing in people, however, is still not as widely accepted a business principle as investing in plant and equipment. The reasons for this are rooted in economic theory and accounting practice.

CAPITAL INVESTMENTS

Traditionally, capital investments in plant and equipment are evaluated over their useful lifetime. For example, to evaluate an investment in a new manufacturing plant, you look at a stream of expenses and revenues over its expected lifetime. On the expense side, it typically starts with a large initial capital expenditure for construction and outfitting, plus continuing expenses for operations and maintenance. On the revenue side is the income stream produced by the plant, typically the projected profits from products produced in the plant. Both the expense and revenue streams are discounted over time to reflect the cost of money (the cost of borrowing for the initial investment). The calculation yields an internal rate of return or a net present value. Companies evaluate these calculated numbers with other alternatives they have for their funds—if the rate of return exceeds those for other investment opportunities, the project proceeds. If not, the investments are made in other, high-yielding projects or programs.

But plant and equipment are not the only form of industrial capital. The other form is known as *human capital*.

HUMAN CAPITAL

Societies invest in people (human capital) in order to increase the society's overall productivity. The primary method of investment is through education and training, although human capital economists have also examined investments in health care and other types of "people" programs.

Economists started looking at investments in people as they attempted to explain the differences in the productivity of different countries, especially between developed and less-developed countries. Their research shows that levels of education within the various countries can be used to explain differences in gross national product (GNP). A separate stream of economic research examines differences in productivity, as measured by earnings, among workers and again found that people with more education generally have higher earnings.

Companies' Investments in People

Companies also invest in their people through training and development programs (as well as health insurance and other employee benefits). The current research on these investments is meager. To apply capital theory to these investments requires the same types of analysis that is applied to investments in plant and equipment. Companies need to examine not only the initial investment in an education or training program, but also the ongoing expenses associated with operations and maintenance. For example, these ongoing expenses might include the time that managers or trainers spend coaching employees on how to apply their newly learned skills. On the revenue side is the revenue stream attributable to the investment—reduced scrap and rework because employees have been trained to make fewer errors. Discounting the expense and revenue streams determines the value of the investment.

DIFFICULTIES WITH EVALUATING INVESTMENTS IN PEOPLE

There are a number of difficulties in trying to apply the same criteria to investments in people as we do to investments in plant and equipment. These include:

- Dehumanizing people.

- Retaining assets.

- Isolating benefits.

- Biases in accounting and tax codes.

- Putting a value on knowledge assets.

Dehumanizing People

Putting people into the same category as plant and equipment dehumanizes the individual. Slaves were classified this way, and were priced according to their perceived lifetime value to their masters. Another calculable investment was indentured servitude, in which individuals were apprenticed to masters in exchange for a fixed period of service. In these cases, the investment model could easily be applied—the slave or apprentice was a factor of production (just like other capital goods). The buyer could calculate the purchase price, the operations and maintenance costs (food, shelter, health care, training, etc.), and the projected revenue stream and evaluate the wisdom of the purchase. In today's society, any mention of these types of practices are met with revulsion (or union activity).

For economists, the measure of a person's worth to a company is generally that person's salary or wages—it is assumed that the person's value to the company is equal to what the company pays him or her to work there. Anyone who tries to calculate the "value of a human being" in any other terms is looked on as a cynic or a lawyer in a negligence case.

> The cynic says that the armed forces know how to place a value on a human life: In a battle, how many men are you willing to sacrifice to save a tank? Divide the cost of the tank by the number of people: the result is the value of the individual.

On the other hand, "investing in people" is viewed positively. Anything that society can do to make people more productive, more able to earn a living and not be a burden to society, is good. The question then becomes *who* should be making these investments: the government, the firm, or the individual himself.

It is generally accepted that the government, representing society as a whole, should make a minimal investment in basic elementary and secondary education and, to a lesser extent, in postsecond-ary education. Few people question the necessity of these invest-ments (although the levels of these investments frequently do come into question as costs, and the resulting tax burdens, continue growing at a rate greater than inflation while the quality of the product appears to be declining). We continue to debate when government responsibility for "grooming productive citizens" should end and the investment burden shift to the company and the individual.

While companies should not classify their employees in the same way as they do their equipment, they must view them as assets—knowledge assets. It is these knowledge assets that will provide the only real competitive advantage in the world economy. And just as with physical assets, knowledge assets require invest-ment and maintenance to make them optimally effective. Accord-ing to Peter Drucker:

> The productivity of knowledge is going to be the determin-ing factor in the competitive position of a company, an industry, and entire country. No country, industry, or com-pany has any "natural" advantage or disadvantage. The only advantage it can possess is the ability to exploit univer-sally available knowledge. The only thing that increasingly will matter in national and in international economics is management's performance in making knowledge produc-tive.[2]

Retaining Assets

Companies that invest in their people have no guarantee that those people will stay with the company. If a company invests heavily in an individual's training and development, that person may be lured to another company that has chosen a different employment and training strategy: rather than invest in training its employees, it will pay more in the market for people who are already trained. Because companies are uncertain about the length of the benefit streams they will receive from their employees, they tend to underinvest in them, even if they believe in their hearts that investing in them is the right thing to do.

> An interesting example showing the perceived importance of both short and long benefit streams comes from LeRoy Roberts, manager of apprenticeship programs at Caterpillar. Caterpillar has been running these programs for decades to supply its factories with trained millwrights, pipe fitters, and machine repairmen. In the late 1970s, they had as many as seven hundred apprentices in the program just in the Peoria, Illinois, area. Since Caterpillar has downsized from ninety thousand to fifty thousand employees over the past several years, the size of the apprenticeship programs has shrunk to 160 people today. And because the company has not done any outside hiring since 1988, today's apprentices come from the base of existing employees, meaning that while in the late 1970s the average apprentice was in his twenties, today they are about forty years old. This means that the expected benefit stream from the investment the company is making in the program has been shortened by twenty years.
>
> How does Roberts justify the program investment economically? The answer is that he doesn't need to—the company views the program as a necessity to fill projected manpower needs. Therefore, the company has never required a separate economic justification of the apprenticeship program.

Companies should be focusing on how to retain their knowledge assets, rather than avoiding investments in their people because of uncertainty about the length of the benefit stream. Many managers believe that their investments in employees have been a primary factor in increasing employee loyalty and reducing turnover. Workers who feel that their companies are investing in their future and empowering and trusting them, are indeed more loyal to their employers.

> David Hogg, manager of continuous improvement/TQM for OCAM Limited, part of the Giffels Group, an international construction and manufacturing consulting firm based in Toronto, tells of a conference he attended on employee empowerment. "In one session, a factory worker from Northern Telecom took out his wallet and removed a corporate American Express card and a Bell Canada telephone credit card. As he waved them in the air, he asked, 'How many factory workers have these?'" He was very proud of the fact that his employer had asked him to be a trainer of other factory teams and, since this role required him to travel to other plants, had entrusted him with these company credit cards. As Hogg tells the story, he comments, "This is going to be a loyal company employee forever."

Nurturing employee loyalty through training and development, employee empowerment, and trust will help companies ensure that they will be the beneficiaries of the full length of the benefit stream being generated by their employees. This is one of the reasons the term "personnel" increasingly has been replaced by "human resources."

Isolating Benefits

It is often very difficult to isolate the benefits directly attributable to a specific training program. The five foundations for the learning organization, for example, are so interdependent, so supportive of each other, that one cannot really separate out the specific benefits of a single team training program. Team training, no matter how good the program content may be, cannot be effective without leadership, without the participants having a set of basic skills, without the overcoming of functional myopia. These other factors can have as much effect on the payback from team training as the training itself. Given that all of these transformation initiatives are so complex, requiring so many different types of training, changes in management practice, and more, it makes better sense to do the economic evaluation on the entire program, not on isolated elements.

When designing a new model, for instance, a car manufacturer doesn't question whether the car should have wheels and tires—they are a basic requirement for all cars. People within the company who specialize in wheels and tires evaluate wheel and tire alternatives to ensure that they match the suspension and other related characteristics of the car. They also look at alternative suppliers and designs, measuring the cost and effectiveness of each. But the wheel and tire department is not asked to separately evaluate the company's investment in the new model's wheels and tires. The economic evaluation is done on the *overall* investment in the new model, wheels and tires being only a small part of that investment.

> So while LeRoy Roberts is running Caterpillar's Machine Repair Apprenticeship Programs without having any firm economic justification other than "we need it to keep the plants running," Jim Despain, vice president and general manager of the Track-Type Tractor Business Unit, is looking at the bigger picture, evaluating the overall costs for machine maintenance and repair. He plans to do an economic evaluation of two alternatives: continuing the apprenticeship program and current practices for maintaining factory machinery or outsourcing machine maintenance to

a third-party supplier. This would shift the training burden outside the company. The question is not the specific cost of the apprenticeship program, but the overall cost of maintaining production machinery in his plants.

Biases in Accounting and Tax Codes

Neither the generally accepted accounting principles (GAAP) nor the guidelines of the American Institute of Certified Public Accountants (AICPA) allow companies to account for training and development costs as capital investments. Similarly, the United States tax laws do not allow companies to account for such costs as investments. This means that even though expenditures on training and development, like other capital investments, are made to provide a stream of benefits over time, they must be accounted for as current expenses, in a category similar to copier paper or cleaning supplies.

Writing in *Training* magazine, associate editor Beverly Geber emphasizes the need to value human resources: "Consider the story of Seymour Cray, says Donald Curtis, a partner in the accounting firm of Deloitte & Touche, in his 1990 book *Management Rediscovered*. Cray was the top engineer and visionary for Control Data, the *Fortune* 500 company that once was the world's only manufacturer of supercomputers. Disgruntled by the company's reluctance to pursue one of his projects, he left one day with some other Control Data engineers to form Cray Research. Assuming that no major financial transactions took place that day, the accounting system recorded that nothing happened. But that defection marked the beginning of a spiraling decline for Control Data, which no longer makes supercomputers."[3]

Changes in the tax codes and accounting principles, including some type of tax credit for investments in employee training and development, have been discussed for many years, but with no real action by any governing body. The lack of such regulations or principles puts training and development budgets at a disadvantage with investments in other types of capital goods that can be depreciated over time. This is one of the major reasons why training and development are often among the first expenses cut by many companies in hard times—with no tax benefit and no immediate payback, training and development programs are an easy target for the budget ax.

Valuing Knowledge Assets

In many industries, the value of a company's knowledge assets can far exceed the value of physical assets. Drug patents are a key asset for pharmaceutical companies. Similarly, chip designs for a computer manufacturer, lines of software code for a software house, CAD drawings for an equipment manufacturer, and so forth, all are key assets. These key assets don't show up on the companies' balance sheets—there is no real way of placing a dollar value on them. Still, the fact remains that without these knowledge assets and the companies' investments in the people who produced them, the companies would be out of business.

Recognizing the value of knowledge assets can change a company's entire orientation toward making investments. Alcoa president C. Fred Fetterolf puts it this way: "Our engineers have really been capital managers."[4] They have been spending pots of money on machinery and not enough on improving brainpower and processes. To change that, companies have to pay more attention to their investments in organizational learning.

INVESTMENTS—NOT COSTS

Company expenditures on training and development programs must be viewed as investments, not current costs. Building a new manufacturing plant requires a large initial investment with the benefit stream starting at zero and slowly building over time. The same pattern holds true when investing in people, as illustrated by the "learning curve."

The Learning Curve

The well-known "learning curve" is shown in figure 7.1—but with a modification. In this learning curve, there is a period of *negative* productivity. When a new plant is built, money and time is spent on construction—so money and time must be expended for training and development programs. The costs include the actual expenditures for trainers, materials, facilities, participants' travel and expenses, plus the cost of having the participants away from their jobs—paying them for "unproductive" time. Once the program is completed, the participants will not immediately display all of the new behaviors or practice all of the new skills to increase their productivity. Just as a new plant needs time to start up, to test new equipment, to have employees learn their way around, so people need time to test their new skills, to learn from applying new behaviors on the job. As time passes, productivity increases, just as new production capacity in the plant builds.

Given that the benefits of training are downstream from the costs incurred, training must be defined as an investment, rather than a cost. For the new manufacturing plant, no one expects it to recover all costs immediately upon commencing operations. Similarly, if training is evaluated strictly on a short time frame, it will almost never show a positive return.

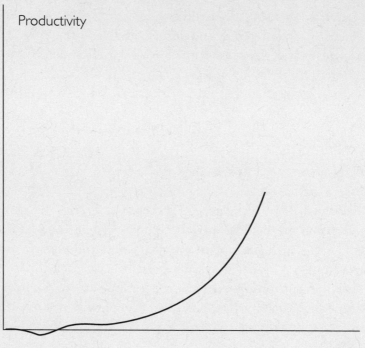

Figure 7.1
The Learning Curve

PEOPLE—THE KEY TO TRANSFORMATION

The key to any successful corporate transformation is in the company's people. The five foundations of the learning organization are all related to people—people acquiring new skills, learning new ways of working, developing new ideas and methods to improve the company's business. According to Robert Reich:

The future prosperity of America and every other industrialized country will depend on their citizens' ability to

148

recognize and solve new problems, for the simple reason that processes which make routine the solution to older problems are coming to be the special province of developing nations. Industries of the future will not depend on physical "hardware," which can be duplicated anywhere, but on the human "software," which can retain a technological edge.[5]

The Role of Technology

Technology is only as effective as the people who use it. Technology can enable and facilitate the types of transformations under discussion, but it cannot cause transformation to take place. Only people can cause transformation. Computer and telecommunications networks can enable and facilitate communication among different functions and organizations, but unless the people are committed to communicating, all that latest technology will sit unused. CAD/CAM workstations and software, for instance, can enable design engineers and manufacturing engineers to share drawings and ideas throughout the development process, but unless the engineers themselves have overcome their functional myopia, they will not allow anyone else to view their work until they feel it is "ready."

In the mid-1980s, I was manager of education and training for Digital Equipment Corporation's Networks and Communications Group. Digital, at that time, had created a competitive edge in the market with its networking technology. I had suggested to my manager that we sponsor a cost-benefit study of our networking technology to provide additional marketing ammunition.

None of the many top industry consultants and business school professors with whom I discussed the project wanted to touch it. The reason? No one felt that the benefits could be quantified sufficiently to show a positive ROI. Networking technology could enable many beneficial business practices—instantaneous communications among worldwide business teams, avoidance of duplication of effort by maintaining and sharing a single database, the establishment of real-time links with customers and suppliers, and so on. But whether any of these practices became real depended less on the technology than on the willingness of people to work together. The technology alone had no worth—the value was created by the people who used the technology. And all of the high-priced consultants and professors said that trying to tie the people side into the calculations made the task all but impossible.

In today's global economy, technology can be bought and installed anywhere in the world in a matter of days. The key to competitive advantage lies not in easily duplicable technology, but in the uniqueness, training, and skills of the human resources. According to Northern Telecom vice president James Marchant, "Busy fingers work eventually leaves Canada and the United States because we cannot compete with the lower labor costs offshore." In North America, Northern Telecom focuses its work on the high-level skills unique to the North American labor market. And it recognizes the need to invest heavily in training and improved work methods to ensure that the human productivity here matches the higher labor costs in this market.

Dan Lawson, quality manager for Blount Canada Ltd., says that "it is the people who make the difference." He illustrates the point with this example: "For several years, we had included a new, million-dollar press in our capital budget requests. The new press would give us added capacity to stamp out parts [for the chain saw components and assemblies they manufacture]. Each year, the request was turned down [because the sales projections didn't justify the investment at that time]. Over the same period, we continued working on improving work methods, machine setup procedures, and preventative maintenance schedules. This year, we took the request out of the capital budget because we have been able to improve the press line's productivity so much that we can handle even more production with our existing machines."

Blount's solution to its capacity problem came from the skills and ingenuity of the people who operate the machines, rather than from investing in new technology.

INVEST IN TOTAL PROGRAMS —NOT ISOLATED COMPONENTS

Companies should *not* invest in:

- Training and development.
- New technologies.
- New plants and equipment.

Companies should invest only in comprehensive approaches to improve their current and future business prospects, and these comprehensive approaches must include *all* of the above elements. Viewing any of the components in isolation will result only in fragmented approaches that can almost never be optimally effective or economically justified.

At Corning's Erwin, New York, ceramics plant, managers tried to radically change the way work was done. They eliminated over twenty different job classifications, leaving only one. Teams were formed and empowered to make decisions about how work was done on the shop floor. As reported in *Fortune*:

> The results were decidedly underwhelming. Productivity suffered, interpersonal squabbles flared, and confusion reigned. Nobody knew who was responsible for what. Says plant manager Gary Vogt: "We took steps to empower [our workers], but the desired outcomes were not reached because we had not prepared them."[6]

In company after company, the stories are repeated. According to human resources and training and development managers:

- Their departments are underutilized by top company management.

- The CEO doesn't know they exist.

- They could really help the company achieve its business objectives if given a chance.

At the same time, these companies' CEOs state:

- They are committed to developing the company's people.

- They never hear from their training and development people.

- Their training and development and human resources departments don't understand the company's business.

It is time that the two groups start talking and working together to ensure that all company investments in new programs include both human and physical capital, and knowledge and technology assets. The subject can be initially broached by either group or through the assistance of an internal or external consultant. Companies must recognize that it is their people who are the key to any transformation effort, that it is the company's unique knowledge assets that are the key to future success.

There are many ways of investing in human capital, formal education and training programs being only a subset of the possibilities. Just as people have created new industrial technologies, many of these technologies have yielded new ways of facilitating learning and the sharing of knowledge. Knowledge is a unique asset: you can give it to someone else and still retain it yourself.

KEY POINTS

Companies must view the costs associated with building the foundations for the learning organization not as current expenses, but as investments whose value will grow over time. In today's competitive global economy, technology can be replicated almost instantaneously anywhere in the world. The knowledge of the company's employees therefore becomes the company's competitive edge.

Investment in people must be considered as part of the overall investment in the company's future, not as an end in itself. Isolating expenditures on training and demanding that they show a high yield doesn't make sense when training is only one part of the company's overall transformation efforts. It is the investment in the overall transformation program that must be evaluated, including training, technology, plant, new work methods, and so forth.

Too often, companies facing a fiscal crisis look to the training budget as one of the first to be cut. This myopic view ignores the fact that it is the company's people who are going to turn the crisis around, if it can be done. In their book, *The Virtual Corporation*, William Davidow and Michael Malone summarize this idea:

> Beyond the fast cycle times, the lean production techniques, the implementation of new communications and data processing, after the new supplier/manufacturer/customer relationships, the adaptive organizations, and the revolutionary products, the virtual corporation comes down to the individual worker. If that man or woman has not signed on to the new business revolution, has not ratified the company's philosophy and accepted its terms of lifelong training, perpetual change, and greater responsibility, then . . . no amount of new equipment or management posturing will make the slightest difference. Without the proper worker, the virtual corporation cannot even be created, much less endure.[7]

EIGHT

EMBRACING NEW WAYS OF LEARNING

In the musical *My Fair Lady* (based on George Bernard Shaw's play *Pygmalion*), Professor Henry Higgins undertakes the transformation of Eliza Doolittle, a streetwise flower girl from the lower classes, into a person whom he can pass off as a duchess by speech and manner. The play tells of Higgins' hard work in training the girl and how, at the embassy ball, Eliza does indeed fool everyone. When Doolittle, Higgins and his friend Colonel Pickering return from the ball, he triumphantly proclaims, "I've done it!" while Eliza sits and fumes. When she angrily flings his slippers at him, he is shocked and asks if anything is wrong.

> LIZA. Nothing wrong—with you. I've won your bet for you, haven't I? That's enough for you. *I* don't matter, I suppose.
> HIGGINS. You won my bet! You! Presumptuous insect! *I* won it.[1]

What Professor Higgins didn't recognize, or want to recognize, was that no matter how great (or poor) a teacher he might have been, nothing could have been accomplished unless the student was able and willing to learn. Higgins presumed that Eliza Doolittle was totally without learning, and that without his expert tutelage, she would remain what he presumed she had always been: a worthless, ignorant, "guttersnipe."

Learning does not just take place in a formal instructional setting, with structured lesson plans and strictly defined teacher and student roles. People learn continuously throughout their lives. Learning is a natural act.

Certainly, formal instructional activities have an important place in the spectrum of learning activities, but more important is an environment where people are able, willing, and eager to learn. The best way to create a proper learning environment is to give people opportunities not only to learn, but also to apply their learning to their work and their lives, and to recognize and reward such learning.

FROM RAW DATA TO WISDOM: HOW PEOPLE LEARN

I think of learning as a four-stage activity (see figure 8.1):

- Stage 1: Data gathering.
- Stage 2: Transforming data into information.
- Stage 3: Transforming information into knowledge.
- Stage 4: From knowledge to wisdom.

Learning Stage 1: Data Gathering

Data are facts. They can be numbers, words or pictures, sounds, smells or sensations. Employees gather data from three primary sources: other people, written materials, and observation. Other

Figure 8.1
The Four Stages of Learning

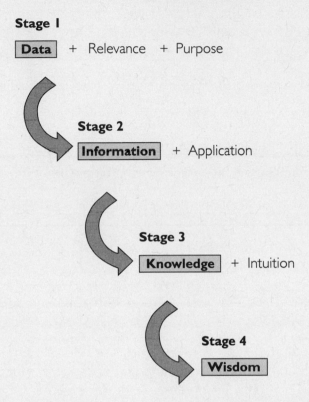

Stage 1

Data + Relevance + Purpose

Stage 2

Information + Application

Stage 3

Knowledge + Intuition

Stage 4

Wisdom

people provide data through formal and informal conversation. Formal conversation can be found in a lecture from an instructor, oral instructions from a supervisor or colleague, or an audio- or videotape or television program.

Formal instruction, whether from a lecturer, a videotape, or a computer-based instructional module, structures data in a way that the instructor believes is logical and that can be absorbed easily by the learner. Formal instruction for an organization's employees is usually given at infrequent intervals. Data are also provided in written form—a textbook, an instruction manual, an interoffice memo, or a display on a computer screen.

People also gather data from observation—watching how things or people work, registering how something sounds, smells, or feels. Data are typically not so well organized in informal and observational situations. Informal data gathering happens constantly, at work and in life in general, through a variety of means.

- Observing a shortcut a neighbor uses to get to work.

- Watching an electrician fix a problem in your house.

- Reading a newspaper article.

- Watching a CPR demonstration on television.

- Listening to other employees discuss their work over lunch.

- Seeing how your supervisor disciplines another employee.

- Listening to how a machine sounds when it is working properly.

But data are relatively useless pieces of information unless the learner has some context for them. For instance, a supermarket's computer contains a lot of data. These data match bar codes on food items with assigned prices. The data themselves are without value until someone uses them—a cashier, a customer, or a store manager—for a specific purpose.

We are bombarded with data constantly. What we want, at least as a starting point, is *information*.

Learning Stage 2: Transforming Data into Information

Management guru Peter Drucker defines "information" as "data endowed with relevance and purpose."[2] For data to be useful to the individual, it must have a context, that is, it must be related to something that the employee finds meaningful. This is why people often retain so little from formal instructional programs; much of the data being thrown at them has no relevance to their jobs or their lives. While they may remember the data (as we do with trivia), they do not transform it into information that they can use.

Consider this scenario: As I place my order on the checkout counter at the supermarket and the items are scanned, the register prints out what I have purchased and the cost of each item. This becomes information for me—how much I am spending, a way of checking that I am being charged the correct price for each item. It also becomes information for the cashier—how much money to collect from me.

The cumulative data are also transformed into other useful information for the grocery store—they use it to check on total sales, sales by item, inventory levels, and the like.

To transform data into information, the employee must make it relevant and see its purpose. Often, an employee will hear something and immediately make a connection to some aspect of her job. This is sometimes called the "Aha!" phenomenon: "Aha! That's why I couldn't do that on my computer" or "Aha! That's why Joe acted that way."

The learning organization not only purposely creates opportunities for its employees to gather data, but also tries to make those data relevant to their employees' work. This ensures that data are more quickly turned into information. Data have no value, information does.

Learning Stage 3: Transforming Information into Knowledge

Information becomes knowledge through its application. An employee may learn some new facts about basic statistics in a formal class. When she relates those new facts to the methods of statistical process control that she needs to use in her job, the data become useful information. But it is only after she has left the classroom and applied that information to her work that she really understands how it works and can say that she truly *knows* it.

When she sees how the statistical methods are applied to the manufacturing processes she controls, and how she can better regulate those processes using those methods, then she has transformed the information into her personal knowledge. It is only at this point that the organization starts to get a return on its investment in her learning, when her knowledge becomes an asset.

Returning to the supermarket example, we see that employees can learn the effect on sales of discounts, coupons, location of merchandise, and so on, from using the information provided by the supermarket's computer. This becomes the employee's knowledge through repeated application—for example, placing a product display at the end of an aisle can increase sales of that product by as much as a factor of 10 times.

An important factor in attaining Stage 3 learning is timing. People are constantly inundated with data and information, but generally retain very little raw data. Unless the data are made meaningful, that is, they are transformed into information, they quickly will be forgotten. Information appears to have a longer life, but to ensure that information is retained, it must be applied—it must be transformed into knowledge. The faster this happens, the greater the learning.

Blount Canada Ltd. has a three-stage process for teaching Statistical Process Control (SPC) to employees. In the first stage, employees take a mathematics refresher course. (If the employee is not successful in this course, he is enrolled in a basic math course offered by the community adult education organization.) These math concepts (data) are immediately made relevant in a forty-hour SPC seminar in which employees learn how to apply them to their work on the factory floor (Stage 2).

Upon completing the SPC seminar, employees are expected to apply the information to their jobs. Blount's Quality Department has two full-time facilitators who not only teach the courses, but also work with employees after the seminar to ensure that they understand the concepts and apply them properly to their work processes. This is the third stage of the learning process, in which information is transformed into knowledge.

Learning Stage 4: From Knowledge to Wisdom

The fourth learning stage adds intuition to knowledge and produces wisdom. As you practice your profession, you develop intuition about what will work or what won't work in a given situation, even if it has never been explicitly tried before. It is the workings of our brains that produce these "hunches." This is what makes people superior to machines, what has yet to be successfully "programmed" into any computer—the creation of new knowledge. Our brains take all of the knowledge we have accumulated, together with other data and information that may have been buried in our subconscious minds, and create something new, something that works, but cannot be explained rationally.

When a Blount employee gets a "gut feeling" that something is askew in his piece of the manufacturing process, even though no variation has yet appeared in the SPC charts, and fixes the emerging problem, his actions are based on experience and intuition, not on any "knowledge" that he can teach another person.

I call this "wisdom." You cannot give anyone wisdom, but you can create a learning environment that nurtures the development of wisdom. This environment encourages individual learning, the application of learning to the individual's job, and the sharing of ideas. It also encourages people to test new ideas and take calculated risks without fear of penalty if their hunch proves incorrect.

WHY LEARNING DOESN'T HAPPEN

All learning starts with data (Stage 1). The purpose of a learning organization is to increase the company's knowledge assets by accelerating learning from Stage 1 through Stages 2 and 3, and to provide an opportunity for people to move to Stage 4 (wisdom). But learning opportunities are often missed for lack of:

- Knowledge of available resources.

- Access to resources.

- Permission to learn.

- Permission to apply what has been learned.

Lack of Knowledge of Available Resources

Data and information are generated throughout a company's internal and external value chains. Universities, consultants, professional organizations, industry analysts, and many other external sources also produce mountains of data on a regular basis. But none of these data are useful unless they can be accessed by the right people—those who need the data, who can transform them into useful information and apply that information to their work.

Many companies fail to utilize all of the data within their boundaries because the employees who need the information don't know it exists.

- A design engineer may waste a lot of time and resources designing a new part that a purchasing agent knows is readily available, at a cheaper price, from a supplier.

- A new salesperson may miss an opportunity with a customer because he doesn't know the customer's buying history—data that exist within the company's customer order database.

- A service technician may spend many extra hours trying to fix a customer's problem, not knowing that another service technician at another location has already developed a quick and easy solution to the problem.

Lack of Access to Resources

A lot of the data within many companies' databases isn't used because it cannot be accessed. Sometimes, inaccessibility is caused by incompatible data standards or incompatible systems or software. For example, when a company starts to integrate engineering and manufacturing operations, it is not uncommon for them to discover that the systems and software being used by the two functions are totally incompatible—there just isn't a way to transfer engineering drawings into the systems being used by manufacturing.[3]

Other times, data are not accessible because the people who own or control the data won't allow access. The owner may be a controlling type: "That's my job, not yours. Keep your hands off." He may fear that someone else will "show him up"—make better use of his systems and data than he does himself. Or he may know that his store of information gives him an internal competitive advantage, that others' job performance would improve if he shared the information, so he hoards it to keep that competitive edge.

Risk aversion is another reason why people are denied access. Often, with old data systems that have had many patches over the years, the owner fears it will all fall apart if someone new tries to monkey with the system. Risk aversion may also stem from security concerns—the records may contain sensitive customer information.

Lack of Permission to Learn

Too often, managers won't permit their employees to learn. "Just focus on your own work. There's no reason to be taking time away from your job to talk with those folks over in the next building. You've got all you need right here to get the job done. If you have any questions, just ask me." This view of the world comes from old management paradigms, and bars employees from seeking new data and information that may improve their performance. These types of barriers to learning can also be erected by managers in the other areas: "Thanks for your interest in what we are doing over here, but we're just too busy with our own work to get involved in yours."

> MIT runs a very successful "Leaders for Manufacturing" program, sponsored by a number of large manufacturers. The program deals with issues surrounding manufacturing leadership, from the viewpoints of both manufacturing technology and management. In speaking with the Digital Equipment Corporation liaison to the program, I asked how Digital uses the information coming from the program. He told me that the information is widely disseminated within Digital's manufacturing organization—to help manufacturing managers make better plans for the future and to generally improve Digital's manufacturing operations.
>
> I asked Digital's program liaison if the information

from the program is routinely shared with the marketing groups responsible for Digital's manufacturing-related products and services. The answer: "No. This is a manufacturing program, not a marketing program."

Digital's return on its investment in the program could be greatly increased if he realized that information on future trends in manufacturing technology and management would greatly benefit others in the company who focus on creating products and services for those markets. But this person's myopic view of the program and his job bars this from happening.

Lack of Permission to Apply
What Has Been Learned

When employees learn, with or without permission, and then try to apply this learning to their jobs by trying out new work methods, managers often block their way: "That's not how we do things here. We've been very successful with the methods we've been using for the past dozen years, and I don't see any reason to change now." This type of behavior obstructs the employee's attempt to apply his learning—to turn the information into knowledge. As employees receive these messages from their managers, they often give up trying to apply their knowledge: "Why bother? The boss is just going to say no."

If you can overcome these barriers, you then have to focus on the optimal ways of introducing learning to your employees' regular work routines.

LEARNING METHODS

Learning isn't something you do for five or ten or twenty days a year when you go off to a training program. It is something you do every day as part of your primary job responsibilities. Too often, when people discuss learning in companies, they think only of formal education and training programs. These certainly have an important role to play in the learning organization, but even more important are less formal methods of learning. The key is to create a *learning environment*, in which employees constantly pursue learning.

There are many companies that spend millions of dollars on formal programs, yet never become learning organizations. They have erected all of the barriers to learning just discussed, and have not built the foundations for the learning organization, have not created an effective learning environment.

CREATING A LEARNING ENVIRONMENT

The five foundations for the learning organization together create a proper learning environment:

■ **Foundation 1: Visible Leadership**
In the learning organization, leaders encourage people to learn and to apply their learning to improve their own and the company's performance.

■ **Foundation 2: "Thinking" Literacy**
In the learning organization, employees have the skills they need both to do their jobs and also to learn how to improve their own and the company's performance.

■ **Foundation 3: Overcoming Functional Myopia**
In the learning organization, employees understand the overall flow of work processes and their roles in those work processes. They work to optimize the overall processes, rather than focusing strictly on local goals and standards.

■ **Foundation 4: Building and Sustaining Effective "Learning" Teams**

In the learning organization, effective teamwork within and across functional and organizational boundaries enables employees to learn from each other and optimize overall company resources.

■ **Foundation 5: Managers as Enablers**

In the learning organization, managers facilitate individual and organizational learning by helping to break down barriers to learning and by ensuring that employees have the skills and opportunities needed to further individual and organizational goals.

The following three program examples, from General Electric, Digital Equipment Corporation, and the Great Lakes Composites Consortium, demonstrate how various combinations of the five foundations can work together to create a learning environment.

GENERAL ELECTRIC'S "WORK-OUT PROGRAM"

General Electric developed its "Work-Out Program" as a structured methodology to involve all of its 300,000 employees in its vision of becoming a "boundaryless organization." The goals of the program included building trust with all employees, empowering employees to share their knowledge and make positive changes, eliminating unnecessary work, and defining and nurturing the vision.

Begun in 1988, the first Work-Out sessions resembled New England town meetings, bringing together thirty to one hundred employees from a single business unit for three days to discuss their common problems. To make certain that communications would be open during these sessions, managers were barred from all but the final sessions. At the final sessions, workers presented their ideas for improvements and managers had to make on-the-spot decisions to accept or reject the ideas. When an idea needed more study, managers were given thirty days to reach a decision, but 80 percent of the decisions were made on the spot.

University of Michigan professor Noel Tichy, who helped to design the process and facilitated some of the sessions, says that a lot of the early sessions started out as gripe sessions. "But in the course of complaining [General Electric employees] also would identify a lot of problems that could be fixed without too much effort. Picking such 'low-hanging fruit,' as GEers called it, was a way to build momentum and trust in a hurry."[4]

Tichy and *Fortune* magazine writer Stratford Sherman repeat a story told by a GE middle manager that illustrates the types of gains GE experienced through Work-Out.

> "We were getting screws from one supplier that were not so good. The bits would break off the screw heads, and scratch the product, and cut people's hands—we had one guy get eighteen stitches. Tempers flared, but management never fixed [the problem]. . . .
>
> "So a shop steward named Jimmy stood up at Work-Out and told the story. This guy was a maverick, a rock thrower, a nay-sayer. He wanted to test us, to see whether we really wanted to change.
>
> "He knew what he was talking about. And he explained the solution, which had to do with how deep the bit could be inserted into the screw head.
>
> "We listened, and then said, 'Okay, what do you suggest?'
>
> "And he replied, 'We need to go tell the supplier what the problems are.'
>
> "Well, I was nervous about it, but I decided to charter a plane to fly Jimmy and a couple other guys to the plant in Virginia where they made the bad screws. . . .
>
> "Jimmy got the problem fixed, and it sent a powerful signal to everyone here. He became a leader instead of a maverick."[5]

GE's Work-Out and the Foundations

Work-Out is based on several of the "foundations for the learning organization." (This is not to say that General Electric has ignored the other foundations, but only that they didn't come into play in this particular program.)

- *Visible leadership.* GE CEO Jack Welch personally attended several of the early Work-Out sessions to demonstrate his commitment to the program. He has also pushed the program through all divisions and levels of GE, ensuring both comprehensive and consistent application. Having Welch in attendance, while intimidating to some of the senior executives who were running the various sessions, made it clear to the lower-level employees that Work-Out was a serious program.

- *Overcoming functional myopia.* Work-Out covers both single-function and cross-functional, cross-organizational problems. Getting all of the players into a single room to work out their mutual problems and relationships helps overcome whatever myopia may have been present in the various GE organizations.

- *Managers as enablers.* In the early days of Work-Out, it was recognized that managers, especially middle managers, were not enablers, but were impeding progress toward resolving problems. For this reason, they were barred from attending the discussion sessions, and attended the final sessions only to make decisions on whether or not to implement the Work-Out groups' recommendations. The message to middle managers became clear: make the solutions work or get out of the way.

The point of Work-Out is that it empowers employees to share their knowledge and learn from each other. It recognizes that many employees have learned how to improve their own and their organization's performance, but have been blocked from doing so by the old culture and by management practices. Work-Out encourages the application of learning. Jimmy understood what the problem was with the defective screws, but management wasn't listening. By opening up communications, both within GE through the Work-Out session, and with the supplier of the screws, the problem was solved easily.

Work-Out is but one of many programs instituted within General Electric to help it become a learning organization. It is not at all a typical training program, but it is indeed a learning program.

DIGITAL EQUIPMENT CORPORATION'S "NETWORK UNIVERSITY"

During the mid-1980s, I was manager of education and training for Digital's Networks and Communications Marketing Group. With the introduction of local area networks and all of the possible applications, this was an exciting time in the networking field. Digital had developed a set of networks and communications products and services that led the industry and was responsible for much of the company's growth during the mid-1980s.

Given the company's new products and technologies, Bob Murray, manager of the marketing group, needed to find a way to educate the field sales organization about the new products and technologies. In addition, he needed to instill in his salespeople a sense of enthusiasm so they could convince their customers that these products would furnish a real competitive advantage. The problem was that the sales force traditionally had shied away from selling networks because they were technically complicated and weren't a high-revenue area.

Murray's approach was to use a wide variety of methods, by:

■ Making the education and training of field sales and sales support personnel a top priority for all marketing, engineering, and corporate support groups.

■ Building and distributing a good selection of sales tools to facilitate networks selling.

■ Establishing electronic bulletin boards (Videotex systems) and computer-based conferences to distribute up-to-date information and to answer questions.

■ Establishing district network teams, composed of sales, software, and field service support personnel, who would provide a high-level focus for local network sales opportunities.

At an early organizational session for the district network teams, team members requested that the marketing group provide a semiannual weeklong training session to keep them up-to-date on the newest products, technologies, competitive information, and other information they would need, as well as to provide them with needed training on the new products and technologies. This program, which became known as Network University, varied from Digital's traditional education and training programs in many ways. A typical weeklong session had the following characteristics:

■ Five hundred to six hundred participants from sales, software, field service, and corporate support groups.

■ Forty to seventy separate sessions, ranging from one hour to three full days.

■ Seventy-five to 150 instructors, speakers, and panel members from marketing, engineering, manufacturing, strategic planning—any and every internal and external resource we needed to present the material.

- Structured, but informal, opportunities for field personnel to interact with engineers, product managers, strategic planners, and others. These sessions increased the learning of both the field personnel and the corporate groups that typically had limited contact with customers.

- Participants self-selected their own curricula from the many concurrent sessions. At the same time, materials from all sessions were provided to every participant, whether they attended the specific session or not.

Through Network University and all of the other support programs that were put into place, we created a true learning environment, where everyone was encouraged to share their knowledge, ask even the hardest, most embarrassing questions and expect straight answers to those questions.

Digital's Network University and the Foundations

Digital was successful in selling networks in the mid-1980s because it created a unique learning environment for all members of its networks-related businesses. The learning environment included elements from all five foundations for the learning organization.

- *Visible leadership.* Bob Murray was a visionary leader. He formed partnerships with his counterparts in the engineering, manufacturing, and product management arms of Digital's Networks and Communications organization and got them all to buy into the vision. From that point on, we never had a problem with finding the right information—whoever had it, from whatever part of the networks world, provided the information, whether for a piece of marketing literature, a training session, or for a question from the sales organization.

- *Basic skills*. Because networks suddenly became a vital part of Digital's overall market strategy, we had to provide a lot of basic training to people new to the field. While Digital's sales force had typically relied on technical specifications to sell its products, they now found that they had to be more conversant with business issues, so we provided basic training on business issues as well.

- *Overcoming functional myopia*. Murray's coalition of all parts of the Networks and Communications organization was a major step forward for Digital. In the past, engineering, manufacturing, product management, and marketing spoke with each other only when absolutely necessary and worked together even less often.

- *The "learning" team*. The formation of the district network teams helped sales, software, and field service audiences to overcome their own brands of functional myopia to be able to sell Digital's networking solutions more effectively. These teams could have been much more effective if they had received training on team skills, but just their formation was a large step forward for the company.

- *Managers as enablers*. The biggest step forward in transforming the managers within the Networks and Communications Marketing Group was in Murray's insistence that they focus everyone's energies on enabling the field sales organization and the district network teams to sell Digital's networks solutions. Previously, managers had focused on local objectives, with little direction or feedback from the field sales organization.

Digital's cooperative concentration on its networks business during the mid-1980s had many of the characteristics of a learning organization. Learning took place not only among the field personnel who were the targets of all these efforts, but also among marketing, engineering, and product management—in fact, everyone involved in the effort. Engineers and product managers, for example, not only shared their knowledge with the field, but also received a lot of information about what customers were really seeking. The result of all this learning was outstanding business growth for several years in the mid-1980s. The lesson here is that a learning organization can be created in any part of a company, but the advantages accruing from it won't be sustainable unless it spreads to all other parts of the company.

THE GREAT LAKES COMPOSITES CONSORTIUM

The Great Lakes Composites Consortium (GLCC) was formed by a group of companies in partnership with the U.S. Navy to provide technology transfer to, and build composites manufacturing capabilities for, U.S. manufacturers using new composite materials and associated manufacturing technologies. The GLCC's Composites Technology Center includes a "teaching factory."

The Composites Technology Center is designed to assist small manufacturing companies in adopting new technologies. Many small manufacturers simply don't have the resources needed to research new technologies and then to move their employees along the learning curve to adopt them.

Working with GLCC staff, a small manufacturer can assign one or more people to work at the GLCC facility in Kenosha, Wisconsin, to test a new technology and actually design a new product using GLCC facilities and expertise. If the manufacturer decides to adopt the new technology, he can set up his initial production line in or near the GLCC site. GLCC will train the manufacturer's employees and help them master the new manufacturing processes.

When the manufacturer's personnel have moved a sufficient distance along the learning curve, the whole operation can be moved back to the manufacturer's own site.

The Teaching Factory and the Foundations

The teaching factory model not only provides for technology transfer, but also provides learning resources, coaching, and reinforcement that few small manufacturers could otherwise afford. The model is built on three of the five foundations.

- *Visible leadership.* The concept of the teaching factory, being heavily promoted by the National Center for Manufacturing Sciences, of which the GLCC is an affiliate, requires visionary leadership to sell and implement the model. For GLCC, this leadership comes from its entire staff, led by Dr. Roger Fountain, the consortium's president and CEO.

- *Basic skills.* The GLCC focuses on technology-related basic skills. The importance of the GLCC model is that these specialized, materials-related skills are not commonly taught throughout the country. GLCC provides a major instructional resource for small manufacturers that probably couldn't otherwise find or afford the necessary instructional resources.

- *Managers as enablers.* The staff of the Composites Technology Center provides the initial management of the project for the small manufacturer. The GLCC's goal is to transfer the necessary skills and knowledge as quickly as possible to the small manufacturer's team through instruction, demonstration, coaching, and reinforcement.

KEY POINTS

People learn in many ways—I think of it as a four-stage activity. First, data must be gathered—perhaps in formal training sessions, from reading, observation, discussion, and myriad other ways. Second, data must be put into context, related to real life. Third, information must be applied in order to become knowledge, and, finally, intuition is added to knowledge to produce wisdom. To become a learning organization, companies must embrace all modes of learning, in each situation assessing the most effective methods to meet their goals.

All of the five foundations for the learning organization are based on and support learning. Without building strong foundations, no company can succeed in becoming a learning organization. With strong foundations in place, a company can travel as much as 80 percent of the way toward its transformation goals.

NINE

BREATHING LIFE INTO THE LEARNING ORGANIZATION

As the baby left the darkness and security of the womb, the doctor held her by the heels and applied one quick firm spank to her bottom. First, a deep inhaling breath, a gasp, then a loud cry, and everyone breathed easier. The delivery team went through its routine of cleaning and checking the infant before handing it to its parents. The delivery team's job was done; the parents' job was just beginning.

Breathing life into the learning organization is in many ways similar to this scene. The newborn first needs a shock to its system to get it started. Then, it needs constant care and nurturing as it learns about its new world. As time passes, it learns its lessons, makes it own mistakes, and becomes more and more independent of its parents. The parents work hard to nurture its development and they take pride in each accomplishment. They hope that the child internalizes the values they try to teach it as it grows. Eventually, the child will have developed sufficiently to break free from parental influence and start its own life and its own family.

ACTION STEPS

To bring a child or the learning organization to life and raise it properly, you must go through a series of nine action steps:

1. "Do we want a child?"
   Learn about "learning organizations" and decide if this is the direction the company wants to take.
2. "Are we ready to start a family?"
   Assess the current status of the five foundations for the learning organization (leadership, basic skills, overcoming functional myopia, effective teamwork, and transforming managers into enablers) within the company.
3. "How do we prepare for this child?"
   Develop plans to build, or shore up, the five foundations.
4. Conception.
   You've decided that you want the child and that now is the right time to start. So start! This requires that you get the buy-in of all involved parties, both those directly involved in the conception and those who will play a support role (doctors for the baby, consultants for the learning organization).
5. Delivery.
   Bring your progeny into the world. Start with that first spank. Similarly, you need to "kick-start" the learning organization by means of an "act of commitment."
6. Raise the child.
   Develop and deliver needed education and training.
7. Inculcate your values into the child.
   Institute a series of learning practices.
8. Encourage and reinforce learning.
   Provide constant reinforcement of new learning and practices.

9. Let your child amaze you.
   Be constantly open to the new ideas that will emerge as employees are freed to learn and share their ideas.

The nine steps (summarized in table 9.1) should be taken in sequence, attending to the decisions and actions that are a part of each one.

Step I. "Do We Want a Child?"

Before making a commitment to the learning organization, or any other transformation initiative, company leadership must learn what it means to make the journey. Read about learning organizations, in this book and others (see appendix B for additional resources). Attend seminars and symposia on the learning organization. Visit companies that have developed a learning organization. Talk with consultants on learning organizations. Get as much information as you can in the time you have available to make the best, most-informed decision possible.

It is important that the top managers of the company do this background research themselves. Sending a junior person to gather the information and make a recommendation makes as much sense as having your teenage neighbor decide for you whether you want a child. The people doing the research and making the decision should be those people who will have to implement the learning organization. Just as having a child shouldn't be undertaken lightly, so the commitment to developing a learning organization involves costs, risks, and changes in the ways in which the entire company works.

When my wife and I were expecting our child, friends with children all said the same thing to us: "Boy, is your life going to change."

Boy, were they right! Developing a learning organization means that life in your company will never be the same again. Ask these questions:

Table 9.1
**Nine Steps to Breathe Life
into the Learning Organization**

1	Decide if this is the approach you want to take.
2	Assess the current status of the Five Foundations.
3	Develop plans to build or shore up the Five Foundations.
4	Get buy-in from all involved parties.
5	Start with an "act of commitment."
6	Develop and deliver needed education and training.
7	Institute a series of learning practices.
8	Encourage and reinforce learning,
9	Be constantly open to new ideas.

- Is this the right approach for this company? Are there other initiatives that will better fit our goals and our culture?

- Are we willing to make the commitment necessary to make this happen?

- Do we have the time, energy, and resources to develop a learning organization?

If the answers to these questions are affirmative, proceed to Step 2. Otherwise, don't bother even starting the trip.

Step 2. "Are We Ready to Start a Family?"

You read the books on childbirth, parenting, and child care. You assess your financial status and how the child will affect your career. You go through all of the checklists and finally answer the question: "Are we ready to start a family?"

Similarly, you must assess the current status of the "five founda-tions for the learning organization."

- Do we have sufficient leadership in the company to make the learning organization work?

- Do our employees have the necessary basic skills?

- How much do we suffer from functional myopia?

- Do we have effective teamwork in place across the entire company?

- Can our middle managers adapt to the new roles that will be required of them?

Be honest with your assessments. The surest way to sink the ship is to delude oneself into thinking that everything is in place when it isn't or that "we really don't need all that." Often, when managers face the need for transformation, they find that they are too close to the organization to be able to see its problems clearly.

> The vice president of engineering sent her manager of tech-nical documentation to benchmark his operations against another company where, she had heard, they were produc-ing better-quality documentation in half the time and at half the cost. When the visit was over, the manager made his report to his vice president: "The other company has better-trained, more experienced writers than we do. They also have better hardware and software than we use, and the documentation writers work as part of the product devel-opment team from day one. Given the skills and experience of our people, the system we use, and the fact that we don't get any information on new products until they come out of field test, our schedules and the quality of our finished documentation are comparable to the other company. I don't see any need for change."

If you are worried that your company's or your own myopia will blur your view of the real situation, hire a consultant who has twenty-twenty vision. You will never reach your goal if you can't see it clearly.

It is important to realize that you don't need to have all of the foundations in place to start building the learning organization. In fact, few companies will have all five (or even three) of them in place. The act of building solid foundations is itself part of the journey. The old "80-20 rule" applies here: establishing the foundations will get you 80 percent of the way to the learning organization (or any other transformation initiative). The highest-level practices of the learning organization—systems thinking—will add the last 20 percent.

Step 3. How Do We Prepare for This Child?

Having completed your assessments around the five foundations, you now need to develop plans to build those that are missing and shore up those that are substandard. As your plans will include activities related to many different skills, you will need to prioritize the list.

In setting priorities for building the five foundations, I place them in three groups. First, without leadership, nothing will happen. Leadership, as discussed earlier, needs to come from the top of the company if a company-wide transformation is expected, but it can and should also come from many levels of the organization. At the opposite end of the organization chart, basic skills for "thinking" literacy must share the highest priority. Without basic skills, the new methods of learning and working cannot succeed.

Second, overcoming functional myopia is a prerequisite to effective teamwork. There are a number of methodologies you can use to help this along. Remember that overcoming functional myopia also requires attention to cultural, organizational, and functional barriers that have long been in place.

Finally, "effective teamwork" and "managers as enablers" go hand in hand—the building of effective, self-managed teams requires that new roles, inside or outside the company, be found for many managers whose work will be taken over by teams.

Step 4. Conception

Your plans are in place. Now is the time to start. Begin by announcing the new directions and informing your employees, throughout the company, about the journey you are about to jointly undertake. Anticipate common questions:

- Why does the company need to change?
- What is a "learning organization"?
- Why has the learning organization been selected as the appropriate model for the company's transformation?
- How will the program affect my job and the structure of the company?
- What do I need to do?
- What if I find it too difficult to learn and change? What happens to me?
- What's in it for me?

These are all real, legitimate questions that you will need to be prepared to answer. The answers should be honest and straightforward, and they should be given by the company's top managers. This is what leadership is all about. If the top managers in the company are not prepared to play this role, you will need to firm up the "leadership" foundation before even starting this step.

People throughout the company must be convinced that not only will the learning organization lead to a more promising future, but also that without change, the company's future is not bright. People who are comfortable with the status quo need to realize that the status quo just isn't good enough.

> One company's CEO hired a consultant to help him improve the company's operations and profits. Nothing the CEO had tried worked, and he hoped the consultant would have some new ideas. The consultant spent two weeks interviewing people throughout the company, but no one would offer a single suggestion as to how their operations could be improved—everyone believed that the status quo was the best they could do.
>
> As her last attempt, the consultant called a meeting of forty employees, from all levels of the organization. Again, she asked for suggestions of improvements that might be made, and again there was silence.
>
> "All right," she declared. "You're being outperformed on virtually every performance measure by seventy percent of your competitors. Maybe it's the best you can realistically do. Let me ask just one final question: What is the dumbest thing you see being done in this company on a regular basis? . . . And don't even think about mentioning the hiring of consultants."
>
> After the laughter died down, one brave person started to speak. "I'm Joe Smith. I was hired about two months ago to run the shipping room. Being new here, I didn't want to say anything, but we do one of the dumbest things I've ever seen every day down in shipping."
>
> "And what's that, Joe?" the consultant asked.
>
> "It's all the empty boxes we ship."
>
> "Empty boxes? I don't understand. What about shipping empty boxes?"
>
> "As near as I've been able to find out," Joe started, "it's been going on for about two years—from the time the company started its new retail stocking system. Potentially, every

one of our one hundred and sixty retail stores could get a shipment every single day, depending on their previous day's sales and their level of inventory. But, really, we only ship to about one hundred to one hundred ten stores on any given day. The other fifty to sixty stores are shipped an empty box."

"Why is that?"

"From what I've been told, it started with the shipping room manager back then. Because stores were told to expect daily shipments, each store that didn't receive a shipment by noon called here to find out where their goods were. It drove the shipping manager nuts—getting fifty or sixty calls every single day. He tried having the department secretary call each of those stores to tell them they wouldn't get a shipment, but it took her half a day, messages were taken incorrectly, and they still got a batch of calls each afternoon.

"Finally, he decided to meet the stores' expectations— every store would get a shipment every day. If they got an empty box with an empty bill of lading, they knew they weren't getting any merchandise that day. It stopped all the phone calls."

There were a few heads nodding around the room. Someone added, "Sounds like a good solution to me!" and even more heads nodded.

"Joe, you said that the shipping of all those empty boxes was one of the dumbest things you've seen done in this company. I understand what you mean, but let's figure out what this really costs the company."

"More than you can imagine," Joe replied.

"Joe, answer this one question for me, and then we'll do the math on the flip chart at the front of the room. How much does it cost you to ship an empty box?"

"The shipping cost is small—it's empty and doesn't weigh much. But we still have to prepare all of the paperwork, bills of lading, shipping documents, and so on. We then have to assemble the box, paste on the shipping label and the bill of lading. Then we have to take the time to load it onto the truck and pay the minimum shipping charges. Let's say twenty-five dollars per box."

Here are the consultants calculations:

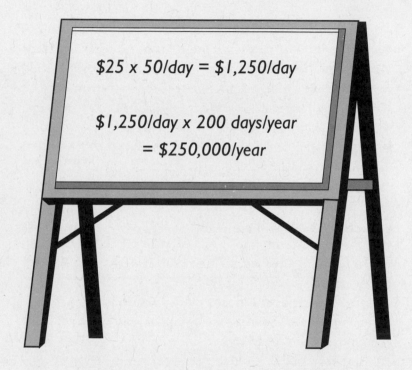

$$\$25 \times 50/\text{day} = \$1,250/\text{day}$$

$$\$1,250/\text{day} \times 200 \text{ days/year} = \$250,000/\text{year}$$

More than a few heads turned when they saw the quarter-million-dollar number. A few whistles were even heard.

"What's the solution, Joe? How much of this money can we save the company?"

"I've done some research on that," Joe replied. "Every store now has a fax machine. The folks in the computer room said that they can fix up my secretary's PC with a fax board. For a couple of thousand dollars, they can write a program to generate and send faxes overnight to all of the stores that won't receive shipments the next day."

"What's the cost of sending the faxes?"

"The investment will be about five hundred dollars for the fax board and telephone interface plus the two thousand for the programming. The calls themselves can be made automatically after midnight to get the cheapest phone rates. Let's be generous with the numbers. The cost per phone call will be at most a dollar. Add another dollar for the cost of operating the fax machine on the other end."

"Let's total it up on the chart in front."

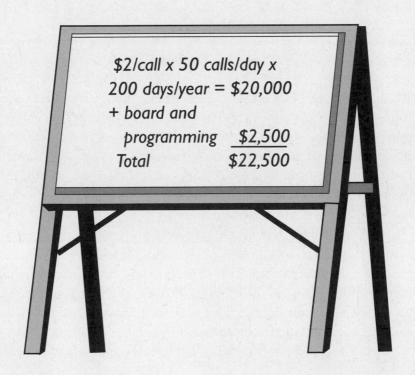

$2/call x 50 calls/day x
200 days/year = $20,000
+ board and
    programming $2,500
Total $22,500

When times are good, people frequently come up with seemingly logical solutions to problems, never bothering to ask if there is a simpler or less costly solution. The issue is resolved and the company is still making money. But as these Band-Aid, chewing gum, and baling wire solutions mount up over the years, you end up with procedures that are so complicated and costly that no one dares touch them for fear of causing a major operational breakdown.

> General Electric CEO Jack Welch talks about all of the extra baggage that was being carried by GE, "the thousands of bad habits accumulated since the creation of General Electric. How would you like to move [out of] a house after 112 years? Think of what would be in the closets and the attic—those shoes that you'll wear to paint next spring, even though you know you'll never paint again."[1]

Step 5. Delivery

It's now time to "kick-start" the program. Just as the infant was introduced to the world with a firm slap to the bottom, so company management must make a clear, definitive *act of commitment* to demonstrate that they are serious about the new approach. Like the farmer and the mule in the old story, while he always treated the mule kindly, he occasionally had to hit it over the head with a two-by-four "just to get its attention."

The best way of demonstrating this commitment is to have top company management do the initial training themselves. Whether you have decided to start with team building or middle management training or any of the other foundations, having top management devote several days of their time to training provides a clear message to all employees that this is important.

If the top company officers are not comfortable doing the

training themselves, they must make a commitment to attend the training with their employees. This also transmits a very strong and clear message: "We are all in this together, and we will all learn together."

There are also other "acts of commitment" that will convey the same message. William Weiss, CEO of "Baby Bell" Ameritech, felt that despite its outstanding current performance, the company would have to change or slowly wither away. As reported in *Fortune* magazine, Weiss felt that "our culture was so strong and so severe that without radical change, our culture would never change."[2] His solution: He created a crisis.

Weiss started by determining which of his top executives he felt shared his vision. Gathering eight of them in an off-site meeting, he gave them the following instructions: "You're a journalist ten years from now. Write the story of Ameritech." Only five or six of the eight shared his views. Those who didn't share his views eventually left the company.

The *Fortune* story continued:

> Then on to the masses. To give the crisis credibility, Weiss told all 70,000 employees what was happening in a few small pockets of Ameritech's business. For instance, by giving better service and prices, some start-up phone companies were stealing Ameritech's business customers. Weiss kept harping on this emerging trend, letting the whole organization know that this was just the beginning of a new competitive world, and that if Ameritech didn't become more customer focused it would lose big.[3]

Whether in a real situation or a manufactured "crisis," the act of commitment grabs the attention of the entire company and demonstrates leadership's commitment to a new direction.

Step 6. Raise the Child

As you raise a child, you teach it basic skills along with independence. You don't punish a child for not knowing how to do something he has never done before—you teach him, allow him to make mistakes, and help him learn from those mistakes until he has mastered each skill.

In developing the learning organization, you must give your employees the benefit of this same approach. They must be given sufficient training in each identified skill area, be given opportunities to practice those new skills and learn from their own mistakes in a reasonably benign environment. People will not take risks to find better ways of working if they fear that their jobs are on the line if they fail.

I had developed a weeklong training program for sales teams. The content of the training was important. Equally important was the need to take the individuals who had been assigned to these special teams and make them feel special—give them some unique folklore that only members of these teams would have. To accomplish this secondary goal, I decided to perpetrate a hoax.

By Thursday evening, the participants were on information overload and were exhausted from the week's grueling schedule of activities. The announced after-dinner speaker was from a government agency and would speak about national and international technical standards. Actually, the speaker was a double-talk artist hired to perpetrate the hoax.

Only my meeting organizer and I knew what was planned, but she thought that the group manager also knew. During dinner, she leaned over to him and said, "This guy's going to be a riot." The manager glared at me across the table and stated firmly, "I want to see you outside!"

When we arrived in the hallway, he asked me what was

going on. I told him about the hoax. His reply: "You know that you are risking taking this incredibly effective week of training and flushing it down the toilet." I told him that I knew what I was doing (and prayed that I was right).

The speaker was marvelous, and no one laughed harder than my manager. At the end of the evening, he told me, "That's the kind of risk I want you to take! You've really created some folklore for the group."

The problem with this manager was that he encouraged his employees to take risks, but only if they were absolutely certain that they would succeed (yes, that is a very obvious contradiction). If you took a risk and succeeded, you were handsomely rewarded. If you failed, he shunned you until you left the organization.

Just as there are as many parenting methods as there are mothers-in-law, there are many learning methods that can be used in the learning organization to supplement formal training programs. You must provide both formal and informal, both structured and unstructured, opportunities for learning.

At a large industrial manufacturer, there were some excellent formal team training programs. But the trainers complained that there was no opportunity to observe the teams once they left the classroom, no chance to provide any further coaching or reinforcement of the classroom learning.

In talking with other members of the training staff, I was told of another program that used a business simulation to help intact teams gain a better understanding of the business. "Why not," I suggested, "have one of your team trainers attend one or two days of the business simulation seminar to observe how the teams are working? In this way, they could provide some coaching on team skills as a complement to the seminar content."

Step 7. Inculcate Your Values into the Child

In raising a child, you try to instill your own values into the child's thinking and behavior. It has often been said, and it is certainly true, that if you don't like the way your child is acting, you had better examine your own behavior. The same holds true in trying to inculcate your employees' thinking with the values of the learning organization.

Many companies have their own expressions for people who have internalized the company's values. IBM employees "wear blue shorts." Caterpillar employees "have yellow paint in their veins." When the old culture is so strong, it takes extra effort to get employees to change their behaviors to new ways.

You need to keep watch to see if the learning organization is taking hold. Are the company's managers and leaders adopting the new behaviors of the learning organization? Are new ideas for improving the business flowing up the ladder as well as down? Are the managers and leaders themselves participating in learning activities?

Step 8. Encourage and Reinforce Learning

Virtually any company you speak with will tell you that they "encourage learning." In many of these companies, however, the statement is more lip service than reality. How do companies encourage learning? A few examples:

■ **Tuition Assistance Plans**

- ■ Base-level: reimbursement for job-related courses at completion.

- ■ Intermediate level: tuition, fees, and books paid at start of course.

- High-level: tuition, fees, and books paid at start of course for all courses, job-related or not.

■ **Skill-based Pay Systems (pay increases tied to mastery of new skills)**

■ **Company-Sponsored Education and Training Programs**

- May include adult education and college courses offered at company sites (good if done after work hours, better if done during work hours or half during and half after work).

- May include satellite courses offered by National Technological University and several other universities.

■ **Benchmarking—Formal and Informal**

- Include employees from all levels and functions on benchmarking teams.

- Encourage employees from all levels and functions to attend industry and professional conferences where they can compare notes with colleagues from other companies.

- Provide incentives for employees who write papers and make presentations at industry and professional conferences.

■ **Opportunities for Informal Learning and Sharing of Ideas**

- Everyone should eat in the same cafeteria and have sufficient time during lunch to hold discussions.

- Executives should routinely sit down for lunch with employees from their own and other departments to listen and share ideas.

- Conference rooms should be available throughout the company's facilities (not just in the executive offices) to give employees a quiet place to sit and discuss ideas.

■ Learning Reinforcement

- Managers should be trained to coach their employees as they apply newly learned skills and information to their jobs. Coaching should be one of the criteria by which managers are measured and rewarded.

- Employees who have mastered new skills should be given responsibility (and rewarded) for coaching other employees who are just acquiring those skills.

Another vital way of reinforcing the new values and behaviors is demonstrated by how the company hands out rewards. If you are trying to get people to work together in teams, your reward systems should pay more to people who are effective team players. But the rewards do not have to be only monetary. Recognition of employees' achievements toward the organization's new goals should also be given. Handing out plaques for outstanding achievement, having a graduation ceremony for employees who newly acquire basic skills, writing up achievements in the company newsletter (or, even better, having a success story written up in the industry press), are all powerful motivators.

At Northern Telecom, when the company is asked to provide a speaker for a conference on effective teamwork, they send team members from the factory floor. Attending conferences is no longer solely a perk for managers. If the shop floor workers are the ones who have the story to tell, they are the ones who are sent—with the same expense allowances that the company's top executives would receive if they were attending the conference.

Step 9. Let Your Child Amaze You

We mark our children's progress, noting the acquisition of the skills we teach and those they learn in school and other venues. Just as our children occasionally amaze us by demonstrating a new skill for which we don't know the source, so building a learning organization can produce startling results in the company's business.

Along with your stated business goals—improved quality or reduced time to market, for example—you will also note unplanned benefits. If you are successful in your quest, some of these benefits may include:

- Higher employee morale and lower turnover.

- Greater customer satisfaction.

- More innovation, both in improving current work methods and in developing new lines of business.

- Reductions in duplication of effort, time to market, and product costs.

- Increased productivity and profits.

KEY POINTS

The process of bringing the learning organization to life in your company parallels the decision to have and raise a child. As summarized in table 9.1, there are nine steps, starting with the decision to have a child, or to introduce the learning organization, and finishing with the amazing results. Starting with the establishment of the strong foundations needed to support the learning organization and following the steps sequentially will ensure that you have planned your transformation well and are completing each step in the plan.

The learning organization is not something you buy ready to use or just suddenly proclaim exists. It must go through the same developmental steps as any major program. Only by nurturing this development can you "breathe life" into the learning organization and watch it develop, mature, and yield impressive benefits.

TEN

CREATING A VIRTUAL TRAINING ORGANIZATION

Most medium-to-large companies, whether or not they are attempting to become a learning organization, have one or more training groups. Smaller companies probably don't yet have training "groups," but instead have individuals in various functions who have been given responsibility for specific training needs.

There may be a corporate training and development group within the human resources department, a sales training group, a services training group, a manufacturing training group in each plant, and so forth. In most cases, these training groups offer courses, seminars, and workshops, presented by their own professional instructors on a regular schedule to the employees who enroll in them. They may also produce self-paced courses, using a variety of print and other media. The courses are developed professionally, according to strict educational methodologies, and are evaluated by the students at the end of each program.

"Traditional" training and development organizations:

■ Focus on the development of individual skills—the individual employee is the customer for the organization's services.

- Do not regularly participate in the company's planning efforts. Instead, they plan and execute their own programs as a separate, internal support function.

- Are not change agents. When the company's business leaders are planning a major transformation effort, such as becoming a learning organization or adopting TQM, they look to the outside for help rather than to the internal training and development organization.

The traditional training and development organization, if it is to help with its company's transformation initiatives, must first transform itself. These groups usually suffer from the same maladies as the companies they serve, and need to build the same five foundations. They need:

- Strong, visible leadership that works constantly with top company management to help achieve their business goals.

- The full range of basic skills required for thinking literacy.

- Ways to successfully overcome their own functional myopia.

- Effective, empowered, self-directed learning teams.

- Redefined managers' roles—managers as enablers.

THE VIRTUAL TRAINING ORGANIZATION

The Virtual Training Organization model is not meant to immediately, or even eventually, replace all existing training and development groups. Sales training, manufacturing training, and the like, are all important functions that generally do valuable work. But in most companies, existing training and development models and organizations are not up to the job of helping their companies transform themselves. The Virtual Training Organization is designed to take on this new challenge, either as a new organization or a supplement to an existing training and development organization. It also is possible for an existing training and development organization to transform itself and become a Virtual Training Organization.

The Virtual Training Organization is a new approach to corporate training and development that:

■ Is itself a learning organization.

■ Has the capabilities necessary to help transform the company into a learning organization.

The reason for the word "virtual" is that in the learning organization, learning takes place constantly throughout the organization. Training, learning, and knowledge development are not the sole province of the training organization, but utilize resources from throughout the company (as well as external resources). The *Virtual* Training Organization starts with a core staff, but utilizes the best available instructional resources regardless of level, function, or organizational affiliation.

The Virtual Training Organization differs in six important ways from the traditional training and development organization. These differences are summarized in table 10.1.

1. Training and Development's Role

Traditional training and development groups focus on the development of *individual* skills. The individuals taking courses are viewed as training and development's customers.

Training and development is most often contained within the

Table 10.1
**Traditional Training and Development (T&D)
vs. the Virtual Training Organization (VTO)**

	Traditional T&D	**The VTO**
Role in the company	Focus on individual skills	Focus on corporate goals
Expertise	Training and development methodologies	Training and development methodologies *plus* understanding of the company's business
Program content	Generic, individuals skills courses	Tailored business solutions
Methods	Formal courses, seminars, and workshops	Formal programs *plus* consultation, coaching, and facilitation
Staffing	Course developers and instructors	Consultants, facilitators, coaches (developers and instructors optional)
Development/Delivery cycle	Time to follow methodologies	Real-time solutions
Basic model	Academic Research	Policy research

company's human resources department. It defines its own budgets and objectives and is often self-supporting, being required to fund its own budget by the tuition charged to students. Typically, it is not connected directly to the company's business planning process, although it tries to keep watch for new developments that may require new course offerings.

In contrast, the Virtual Training Organization focuses on helping the company, rather than individual employees, succeed. (Of course, individual employees are the ones who learn and who institute new practices, but they are not the primary focus of the Virtual Training Organization's goals.) The Virtual Training Organization participates in company planning efforts and aligns its own objectives with those of the company. It can be housed in any part of the company, but is represented on major business committees, including the company's executive committee.

2. Expertise

In the traditional training and development organization, there is a lot of educational expertise. Its members have rigid standards for the development and delivery of courses. It also has substantial expertise in the subject matter it teaches, such as supervisory skills, time management, career planning, or other individual skill areas.

> In a number of traditional training and development organizations with which I have worked, each developer and instructor has on his bookshelf a thick binder containing standards for design and delivery of courseware. The standards include everything from how to write instructional objectives to page layouts and typefaces for student materials. In some of these organizations, the standards are actually used. In others, they sit on the shelf, being opened only to impress others in the company with the professionalism of the group. Whether or not they are actually used, these standards are local, and do not take into account the needs of the company the group is serving.

Standards of excellence are also important to the Virtual Training Organization. But in the Virtual Training Organization, its overarching goal is to respond in a timely, cost-effective manner to pressing company business needs. In order to meet this additional requirement, the Virtual Training Organization requires that its members also understand the company's business and its operations. Only in this way can it ensure that its programs and services are contributing to company goals.

3. Program Content

The traditional training and development group focuses on creating and delivering courses related to *individual* skills development. While this work is important to any company, the focus on the individual employee blurs the view of the needs of the larger organization.

The Virtual Training Organization provides "tailored business solutions." These solutions may include individual skill development, but also other important services, such as consultation to business managers, organizational design and development activities, meeting facilitation, ongoing coaching and reinforcement of new management styles.

4. Methods

Traditional training and development groups focus on developing and delivering formal instruction through courses, seminars, and workshops. Typically, because of long development cycles and large development costs, these programs focus on generic skills development. In this way, a course can be taught on a regular basis, for many different audiences, so that the development costs can be spread over multiple offerings.

The Virtual Training Organization also offers formal programs, but only as part of an overall plan to support the company's business objectives and priorities. Formal instruction becomes part of an overall game plan that may also include consultation, coaching, and facilitation.

5. Staffing

Traditional training and development organizations are staffed by instructional developers and instructors. The Virtual Training Organization focuses its skills inventory on consultation, facilitation, and coaching skills. Instructional development and training skills may be required at some point, but the Virtual Training Organization has the option to outsource these skills.

6. Development/Delivery Cycle

The traditional training and development organization requires sufficient time to develop and deliver its courses according to its professional standards. One definition of "professionalism" is that professionals are more tied to the standards of their professions than to their employers. Unfortunately, these "professional" goals sometimes keep the group from responding to the needs of their company in a timely, cost-effective manner.

> The company's sales force didn't understand the new products. They were misspecifying solutions, selling solutions that wouldn't work. Customers were rightfully and righteously complaining. The marketing group responsible for the new product set went to the sales training department.
> "We know what the problem is. We have the solution. Here are the new guidelines, a set of common questions and answers, and a straightforward procedure to get the salesperson to the right solution. How fast can you get a half-day course together and deliver it in each of the six U.S. regions?"
> The sales training manager, who had written the procedures manual himself, responded: "We just can't do it that way. We need to start off with a needs assessment to

make sure that we understand the problem. Then, we need to develop instructional objectives, train our developers on your product set—"

"What are you talking about? We have the answers right here!" screamed the marketing manager. "When can you deliver it?"

"Following our procedures, to make certain that the course meets all of our professional standards, we can probably get a pilot ready six months from now—provided, of course, that you can come up with the thirty-five thousand dollars necessary to fund the development effort."

The marketing manager left in a huff, assigned two of his people to the task and delivered the six regional workshops within thirty days and solved the problem. In this case, the marketing manager had created a temporary, but effective, Virtual Training Organization within his own group.

The Virtual Training Organization focuses its efforts on meeting the needs of the company in "real time." "Real time" is a computer-related term, meaning that solutions are derived as problems develop. For example, when an alarm goes off in a nuclear power plant, the problem must be solved in "real time." There is no time available to develop a long-term structured research study—it must be fixed now!

This does not mean that the Virtual Training Organization has no standards for the quality of its development and delivery efforts. It only means that responsiveness to company needs takes precedence over adherence to strict educational methodologies. Other differences between traditional training and development organizations and the Virtual Training Organization can best be explained by examining the set of eight basic principles through which a Virtual Training Organization operates.

EIGHT PRINCIPLES FOR THE VIRTUAL TRAINING ORGANIZATION

There is a set of eight basic principles for the Virtual Training Organization (see table 10.2) that distinguishes it from traditional training and development organizations. These principles can be used in the creation of a new training organization or by an existing training and development organization in its quest to align itself more closely with its company's strategic business directions.

Principle 1. Training Isn't Always the Right Solution

A product manager came to see the sales training manager. "We need to put together a training program for the sales force on our new product set. The products are really terrific, we've done a lot of advertising and have a lot of interest from customers, but the sales force just isn't selling the products. Let's give them whatever training they need."

The sales training manager asked for a few days to look into the problem. Later in the week, he called the product manager. "This isn't a training problem. I've checked with several salespeople and several sales managers, and the salespeople have all the information they need to sell your products."

"Then why aren't they doing it?" demanded the product manager.

"Their goal sheets don't include any goals related to your products."

"What does that mean?" asked the product manager.

"It means that the salespeople are making their quotas and getting their bonuses based on the goals that are on their goal sheets. If you want your products to be sold, you need to get them onto the goal sheets. It's as simple as that."

Table 10.2
**Principles for
the Virtual Training Organization**

1	Training isn't always the right solution.
2	Learning must be relevant.
3	Coaching and reinforcement are part of learning.
4	All employees are potential instructional resources.
5	Timeliness is more important that methodology.
6	People learn in many ways.
7	More learning takes place outside the classroom than inside.
8	"One size fits all" solutions rarely fit well.

Traditional training groups know training. If someone goes to the training department and asks for a training course, they get a training course, whether or not training can solve their problem. In the preceding case, the sales training manager, in a traditional organization, would have assigned an instructional developer who would have gone through the procedures and developed a first-rate sales course on how to sell the product—and the sales force still wouldn't sell it.

The business of the Virtual Training Organization is to help company managers solve their problems. When, through problem diagnosis, the Virtual Training Organization determines that there is a training problem, then a training solution is developed. If it isn't a training problem, the appropriate solution, such as getting the new products onto the goal sheets, is recommended.

Principle 2. Learning Must Be Relevant

There are dozens of supervisory skills programs available in the market, and hundreds more that have been developed by in-house training and development groups, and virtually every one, while well developed and well delivered, contains a large proportion of irrelevant data. Unless the subject matter being taught can be applied immediately to the student's job and help her solve a current or impending problem, the data are irrelevant. And if they are irrelevant, why waste the time and resources of both instructors and students?

The Virtual Training Organization aligns all learning activities with current company directions, with the real work that employees are doing, to ensure that the learning is relevant—that learned data are transformed into information and subsequently applied on the job to transform the information into knowledge.

Principle 3. Coaching and Reinforcement Are Part of Learning

Learning doesn't happen instantaneously. True learning requires that people take enough time and have the opportunity to try out new skills in a protective atmosphere. The transformation of information into knowledge requires that people apply their newly acquired information to the job and learn from their mistakes. In most traditional training and development programs, there is no follow-up to classroom instruction—students finish the course and are left on their own.

In the Virtual Training Organization, coaching and reinforcement on the job are vital aspects of the learning process, ensuring that the learning is applied properly, that there are answers to questions that inevitably arise once the student tries to apply the new information to his work. The measure of success is not how many hours students spend in the classroom, but how successful students are at applying their learning to their work—how much new knowledge is created.

Principle 4. All Employees
Are Potential Instructors

Traditional training and development groups, in most cases, utilize their own instructional staff (or external instructors) almost exclusively. They believe this is necessary to ensure that instructors are properly equipped and trained.

In the Virtual Training Organization, instructors can come from anywhere in the organization—everyone from the CEO to the shop floor worker is a potential resource for helping the company and its employees learn. The primary requirement is that the resource person know the subject matter and be willing to share that knowledge with others. The Virtual Training Organization takes responsibility for teaching or coaching these subject matter experts to ensure that any instruction meets the students' learning objectives.

The role of noninstructional personnel in the learning process is especially important in the coaching and reinforcement phase of learning. Instructors cannot follow each employee back to the job to monitor how each applies the information to his or her work. The people who must do this type of follow-up are the students' co-workers and supervisors (who themselves need to be trained to fill these roles).

Principle 5. Timeliness Is
More Important Than Methodology

The profession of training and development is closely akin to that found in education. The model for educational research, derived from that for academic research, places greater weight on strict adherence to formal research techniques and procedures than on the outcomes of the research. To earn an advanced degree, you must study these research methodologies and complete a major research project to demonstrate your mastery of them. With academic research, timeliness is secondary to methodology. (How many graduate students does it take to change a lightbulb? Only one, but it takes six years).

There is another type of research, *policy* research, in which, while not ignoring questions of methodology, solutions are of primary importance. With policy research, a decision maker might tell the researcher, "I have to make a decision on this matter in two weeks. I want you to get me as much information as possible in that time, so that I can make the best decision possible." With policy research, timeliness is more important than methodology.

The Virtual Training Organization focuses more on the *policy* research model. In today's intensive competitive environment, companies do not have the luxury of time—they cannot afford to spend large amounts of time deciding which path to take.

Benchmarking is a form of policy research. Rather than spending large amounts of time designing and conducting a formal study of a potential new practice (such as the learning organization, TQM, etc.), companies do relatively quick studies of other companies to identify best practices, and then adapt them to their own situations.

In the previous example, where salespeople were selling poor solutions to customers, the company cannot afford to follow a strict set of standards for the development and delivery of training. It must get a few bright people together and have them solve the problem as quickly and effectively as possible. Later, if they find out that their solution wasn't the optimal one, they can go back and make modifications. What they cannot afford to do is wait until the ideal solution is identified and developed.

Principle 6. People Learn in Many Ways

Just as training is not always the solution to a business problem, so formal instruction is only one of many ways in which people learn. People learn from each other. An instructor may be the person standing at the head of a classroom giving a lecture, the person in the next office who shows you how to use a feature on your personal computer, another salesperson who has faced a similar customer situation, or another member of your work team who has an idea to simplify your work.

There are many learning methods, and solutions to learning problems must consider a variety of approaches to determine which will be the most timely and cost-effective. Many traditional training and development groups rely much too heavily on formal, stand-up instruction because it is what they know and what they do.

Principle 7. More Learning Takes Place Outside the Classroom Than Inside

No matter how excellent an educational program may be, no matter how flawless the instructor, the materials, and the setting, at least half of the learning that takes place happens outside the classroom. People learn from each other, through informal conversations, swapping war stories, observing how others do their jobs, and the free, nonjudgmental exchange of ideas. Learning organizations make certain that there are frequent opportunities for these types of exchanges to happen.

- Some companies require top managers to eat lunch in the company cafeteria on a regular basis—not sitting by themselves, but with office and factory workers. This allows for an open exchange of ideas that probably would not have made it "up through channels."

- Many companies, Northern Telecom and Blount Canada Ltd. among many others, are building soundproof conference rooms in factory areas, to give floor workers a quiet place to sit and discuss their work and ideas.

- Top executives in some companies, such as Southwest Airlines, spend a day a month working regular jobs in the companies' retail stores or other operations. In this way, they remember who is really doing the work, interact with employees and customers, and become more grounded in reality.

■ Even when designing a formal educational program, it is wise to allow time, and sometimes provide an informal structure, for the participants to meet among themselves to swap stories and ideas.

■ "Groupware," computer-based software that allows employees, regardless of location, to exchange information and ideas with each other, is one of the most rapidly growing methods being used by companies to encourage the open sharing of ideas.

The learning organization nurtures learning for all employees, at all levels, in as many ways as possible. The opportunities for informal learning outside the classroom are probably more important than any formal training program.

Principle 8. "One Size Fits All" Solutions Rarely Fit Well

There are dozens of training vendors and literally thousands of consultants who are ready to supply your company with any training you believe you need, ranging from team building to leadership to management skills to literacy education. A lot of them have spent years developing excellent materials and have well-trained, experienced instructors.

In some cases, these training programs can be purchased and used "as is." Do you need to train people in how to use their personal computers? Do you need to provide training on basic statistics? These are skills that can be attained through generic training.

In building a learning organization, in building or strengthening the five foundations, you are not dealing with vanilla-flavored training. Training on any of the five foundations must be tailored to your company's culture, organization, and business practices. This is not to say that you have to develop and deliver all of this training in-house. What it means is that any vendor you hire from the outside must tailor his or her approach and materials to fit your company's specific needs and circumstances. "One size fits all" solutions can be good—but only if you happen to be the right size.

Using these eight principles for the Virtual Training Organization, we can now move on and illustrate how you can create one within your own company.

SIX STEPS TO CREATING A VIRTUAL TRAINING ORGANIZATION

Whether your company has one or more traditional training and development organizations, or is creating its first, there is a set of six steps (see table 10.3) necessary to create a Virtual Training Organization to help guide and facilitate your transformation efforts.

The purpose of creating a Virtual Training Organization is to facilitate the company's construction of the five foundations for the learning organization. The six steps in the process, described below, must therefore take place in lockstep fashion with the company's efforts to build or strengthen its foundations.

Step 1. Hire/Appoint a Director for the Virtual Training Organization

The director of the Virtual Training Organization should have a proven understanding of both the company's business and the techniques of making major change happen. This does not mean

Table 10.3
**Six Steps to Creating
a Virtual Training Organization**

1	Hire or appoint a director.
2	Determine the organization's priorities.
3	Develop plans based on priorities.
4	Assemble the right resources.
5	Contract for needed services.
6	Eliminate noncompetitive resources.

that the person must be an expert consultant as well as a master of training and development techniques. Consulting skills are probably most important, and the director should also have an understanding of what training and development can and cannot accomplish. Actual knowledge and experience in instructional development and delivery can be obtained by hiring other staff for the organization.

The director should, if at all possible, come from within the company and bring a reputation for getting things done on time and in a cost-effective manner. The candidates should be aware of the company's challenges and problems, the principles of the Virtual Training Organization, and the objectives being set for the new organization. Most important, the director must be a person who has the trust of top company management.

It is also possible for an existing training and development director to apply the lessons of this chapter to transform an existing, traditional organization into a Virtual Training Organization. In doing this, the director must apply all of the foundations for the learning organization and all of the principles and procedures being discussed here. The new beginning must be publicly announced and all of the leadership principles mentioned earlier must be strictly applied if this type of transformation is to succeed.

In a small company, which does not have any full-time training groups, the director may be a person who starts out with part-time responsibilities for training and development, with the position growing to full-time as the role expands.

Step 2. Determine the Organization's Priorities

Working with top company management, the director (and his team in larger companies) will determine the priorities for the Virtual Training Organization—which challenges are to be faced first, who will be in the intended audience, the necessary time frames, and available budgets. These matters should not be presented to the director as a *fait accompli*, but should be negotiated as part of the company's overall planning process. It is vital that the Virtual Training Organization be represented on the topmost planning committees within the company.

The organization's first programs should have wide visibility, be tied directly to the overall directions of the company, and have specific, measurable success criteria. They should not overlap programs already offered by existing groups in the company.

Step 3. Develop Plans Based on Company Priorities

Once agreement is reached on the new group's first assignment, the director must develop plans to meet the challenges set for the first program. The director should examine internal experiences related to the program and also benchmark with other companies that have done similar programs. Once this "policy" research is done, the director must develop a detailed plan for the first assignment and present it to top company management for approval.

Step 4. Assemble the Right Resources

The director must next assemble the right resources to implement the plan. Since this first assignment will be key in establishing the organization's credibility as a partner in change, great care must be exercised to ensure that the best available resources, internal or external, are recruited.

In building the organization's staff, internal candidates from existing training and development groups, should be allowed to compete for these positions along with other internal and external candidates. The staff should have a balance of education and training skills, along with consultation, coaching, and facilitation skills. They should also demonstrate an understanding of the company's business and of the major issues to be dealt with in the highest-priority programs.

In a small company, the Virtual Training Organization's director may have no staff, and will therefore need to rely on his or her own expertise and, beyond that, to contract for any needed services with internal or external groups.

Step 5. Contract for Needed Services

Assuming that the first programs to be undertaken by the Virtual Training Organization include some education or training components, its staff must contract for their development and delivery. Unless the organization has sufficient personnel to do these tasks itself (which isn't likely, as it has just started operations), it must identify the best internal or external resources for each job.

Existing internal training and development groups should be allowed to compete for the development and delivery contracts on an equal basis with external vendors. This action will make it clear that the Virtual Training Organization has not been created for the purpose of eliminating other groups. At the same time, it will give those internal groups a benchmark for their own ability to compete with the best external vendors.

It is possible that other resources within the company may have the subject matter expertise for the program but lack the experience to develop and deliver a large-scale educational effort. In this case, the Virtual Training Organization can supplement the group's subject matter expertise with its own (or contracted) educational expertise.

Step 6. Eliminate Noncompetitive Program Resources

Over time, it will become clear whether existing internal training and development groups are competitive with available external resources. For example, if you have an internal training group focused on basic skills training, you can compare its costs and effectiveness with services available from the local community college or adult education agency. As the Virtual Training Organization develops new programs and examines the proposals from both internal and external groups, the results of such comparisons will become increasingly clear. When the company finds that internal groups cannot compete effectively with available external resources, the internal groups either should be retrained or dissolved and, where possible, new roles found for their employees.

Some groups will withstand these comparisons well; one that trains new manufacturing employees on how to maintain machinery that is unique to the company will probably continue to exist, for example, because no one else, inside or outside the company, can do the job. On the other hand, if you have three groups doing TQM training with three different, incompatible methodologies, company management should decide which one methodology is going to be used. This will usually mean that two of the groups will prove to be unnecessary. These groups can bid on other work or can be retrained to join the third group, which probably will need more help if it is taking on company-wide responsibility. By setting up these new criteria for education and training activities in your company, it will not take long for the groups to shake themselves out.

THE VIRTUAL TRAINING ORGANIZATION IN ACTION

The following examples illustrate how the principles of the Virtual Training Organization have been used by Corning, Digital Equipment Corporation, and PPG Industries. In the Corning and PPG cases, existing training and development organizations were successful in realigning themselves with their companies' strategic business initiatives. The Digital case illustrates how a new Virtual Training Organization was formed when the traditional organization could not shake itself free of its long-standing practices.

Corning: Using Education to Transform a Company

Several years ago, Corning, Inc., transformed its internal Education and Training Directorate into a Virtual Training Organization.[1] It started with the hiring of a new director, Ed O'Brien, a twenty-three-year Corning veteran and former director of human resource planning and development for the company. O'Brien worked with Corning chairman James R. Houghton and other top company managers to determine the organization's priorities and create a four-part strategy statement:

> *Strategy I:* The directorate will create a lean, purposeful organization by leveraging new technology and external resources to better meet individual training needs.
> *Strategy II:* We will shift our emphasis to focus on areas of high impact requiring fundamental organizational change.
> *Strategy III:* We will focus on the highest corporate priorities.

Strategy IV: We will provide a minimum of 30 percent return on investment as a way of determining the highest priorities for training.[2]

O'Brien inherited a staff of thirty when he took over the training department. To build the organization's staff, he "pushed some of his inherited staff people out of the training department into 'more appropriate' jobs within Corning." At the same time, he hired others, focusing staff capabilities on "three important qualities: broad conceptual skills, customer sensitivity and the ability to be change agents." In all, he downsized the department about 25 percent.

The next decision was to contract out most basic skills training, which had previously been a major focus of the education and training group. Much of this work was given to the local community college and was supplemented with courses from an external training vendor. This allowed the Education and Training Directorate to focus its staff and its work on the higher company priorities: total quality, manufacturing strategy, internal growth, values and philosophy, and return on equity.

What were the keys to O'Brien's success? As reported in *Training* magazine, one key was the directorate's constant testing of itself and its customers. Another key was O'Brien's long experience with the company. He "knew the culture, the managers and their values, [and] was able to bounce program ideas off key individuals and get them invested in the process in a way that built support."[3]

Digital's Network University

In 1984, Digital Equipment Corporation was getting ready to launch the networking strategy that would ensure its success for the next several years. Bob Murray had been hired to set up a new Networks and Communications Marketing Group that would lead the charge into the market for the upcoming set of local area networks strategies, products, and services.

At that time, I was the strategic planner for networks training within Digital's educational services organization, a large, traditional training and development organization, which developed and delivered both internal and customer training. This job entailed planning strategies and programs for all internal audiences on Digital's networking products and services.

Working with the marketing organization, as well as engineering, product management, backup support groups, and the field sales and sales support organizations, I developed a radically new approach to the training of field-based networks personnel. When presented with this new approach, top educational services management said that it "was not the way things are done in educational services."

I took my proposal to Bob Murray. He read it and liked it. "Go do it!" he said enthusiastically. I explained the problem to him: "Educational services won't support the proposal. It doesn't follow the models and procedures they always use."

Murray immediately picked up the phone, called my manager, and hired me. I already had spent a lot of time determining the organization's priorities—they were the basis of my program proposal. The challenge now was how to start implementing the plan. Murray made it clear that this was going to be a one-person organization.

At his next staff meeting, Murray asked me to propose a pilot program that would respond to a high-impact training need. I immediately suggested training on our major competitor's product: IBM's Systems Network Architecture (SNA). There were several reasons for this choice:

■   Digital's network architecture was in direct competition with IBM's SNA. Our sales and sales support people needed to understand it in order to compete against it effectively.

■ Digital was also selling a set of products that cooperated with IBM's SNA. Unless our sales and sales support people understood SNA, they could not explain the benefits of the Digital approach to their customers who were using SNA.

■ I had been trying unsuccessfully for more than two years to get educational services to do SNA training. Every request was refused for two reasons: (1) Digital did not do training on competitors' products, and (2) there was no expertise on SNA in the educational services development group.

Murray turned to his manager of product marketing and when she concurred on the need for my plan, he told me to go do it.

A network engineer had described to me a two-day SNA seminar he had attended. Sponsored by a major technical training vendor, the seminar was given by an independent consultant whose expertise was in SNA. The engineer strongly endorsed this consultant, with whom we contracted to give his two-day seminar at Digital.

At the same time, I worked with marketing, product management, and engineering personnel to develop a third day of training that would compare and contrast the IBM and Digital approaches, describe the Digital products designed to cooperate with the SNA environment, and provide guidance on when to compete and when to cooperate with the SNA environment. Within the next ninety days, we offered the three-day course three times, to a total audience of more than 250 people, at a direct cost of approximately $15,000. The ratings of the course were outstanding. If I had ever been successful in convincing educational services to develop this course in-house, the development cost alone would have exceeded $100,000, it would have taken more than a year to develop, and the staff instructors would not have been as knowledgeable about the subject matter as the external consultant and the internal subject matter experts from marketing and engineering.

This eventually led to the creation of what became known as Network University, a semiannual training program for Digital networking sales and sales support personnel from around the world. Still recognized as one of the most effective training programs ever delivered within Digital, a typical Network University session involved hundreds of students attending dozens of different sessions given by subject matter experts. At each semiannual, week-long session, 80 percent of the content was new. All of this was done with a training staff consisting of myself, a meeting planner, and, later, another professional.

The creation of a Virtual Training Organization was what made Network University possible. The program could not have been done under the existing guidelines within Digital's traditional training and development organization.

Re-creating Training at PPG Industries

As PPG Industries started moving "from a traditional reliance on commodity-based industrial manufacturing—glass, fiberglass, chemicals, coatings, and resins—to a more flexible mode of customer-driven specialty marketing," the training, development, and education group "carefully examined its goals, strengths, and potential contributions to organizational objectives."[4]

The group had grown up as a traditional training and development organization, focusing on the individual employee as its customer. It had measured its success by how many students took its classes, rather than on any effect its programs had on the company's business. After much analysis and soul-searching, training, development, and education decided on three new objectives for its business:

To align its performance with business-unit operations.

To ensure that its products and services added value.

To gauge its effectiveness through measured results.[5]

Having defined this new role, training, development, and education director Stephen McIntosh presented the plan to senior line and staff vice presidents and received their enthusiastic endorsement. To ensure that the organization would stay aligned with the company's business directions, it assembled a "training-leadership board" composed of business-unit leaders and chaired by a member of the company's management committee.

As the organization's seven staff members have approached the company's business managers on a proactive basis (rather than sending them course catalogs as in the past), they have been enthusiastically received. McIntosh says that most of the business managers have been "pleasantly surprised" by the new roles of the training, development, and education staff and continue to discover the value that the organization can add to their business planning and implementation.

These role changes require the staff to play a more active role in working with business-unit managers, advising them on how the organization could help them meet their business objectives. At the same time, staff members started following company-wide business practices in planning and running their own business. This has required that the training staff themselves learn more about the company's business and learn how to run their own organization as a business, rather than a support unit. For example:

Within one course area, a [training, development, and education] product manager tries to meet specific customer requirements by customizing the training material as needed. Training design and facilitation are still critical, but such aspects as customer involvement, internal marketing, price competition with external suppliers, and product delivery have taken on new importance.[6]

Keys to Success at Corning, Digital, and PPG

There are several key points to make about the successes of these three organizations.

- *Leadership.* These training organizations not only had strong leadership themselves, but also had support from corporate leadership, in Corning's case from the chairman, James Houghton, in Digital's case from marketing manager Bob Murray, and from business unit managers in PPG Industries. Murray had also formed a series of key partnerships with his counterparts in Digital's networks world, so that there was never a question whether key individuals from engineering, marketing, product management, and other groups would be available to develop and deliver the needed training.

- *Alignment with corporate priorities.* In all three companies, the training groups worked hard to ensure that all of their work was closely aligned with corporate directions and major priorities. There was no "business as usual"—programs were continually renewed and revised to match today's and tomorrow's agendas.

- *Costs and return on investment.* At Corning and Digital, the cost of training on a per-student basis actually decreased from what it had been, at the same time providing greater returns on the company's investments in education and training. In all three cases, business managers were more willing to make investments in education and training because they saw real returns on those investments in terms of their achieving their own objectives. At PPG, according to training, development, and education director Stephen McIntosh, "we continue to evolve measurement techniques to cost-justify each program."

■ *Leveraging internal and external resources.* In all three cases, the training groups have not greatly expanded their staffs, but have relied on leveraging internal subject matter experts and external consultants and vendors to meet their companies' learning needs in a timely manner.

Creation of the Virtual Training Organization can be accomplished at the corporate level or, as in the Digital case, at the level of a strategic business unit (SBU). In either case, it can have a major impact on the company. But just as companies seeking to build a learning organization must expect and embrace continuous improvement, so must the training organization.

The challenge for the future, as Ed O'Brien sees it, is "to have an aggressive program for continuous improvement and to be poised to meet the inevitable changes driven by global competition."[7]

KEY POINTS

Creating a Virtual Training Organization to help the company build or strengthen the foundations for the learning organization requires a whole new orientation for traditional training and development groups. Rather than offering a series of courses to develop individual skills, the new model requires the training group to become directly involved in the company's business planning and to tie its programs and activities directly to the achievement of those objectives. It also requires that the training group organize, manage, and measure itself using the same business criteria as the rest of the company: product quality, customer satisfaction, continuous improvement, and return-on-investment.

The traditional performance measures for training and development have been how many courses are offered, how many students go through those courses, and how students rate the instruction offered. The new model requires that training, just like other departments within the company, measure not for activity levels, but for results.

ELEVEN

MEASURING FOR RESULTS

In today's tough economic environment, managers want to ensure that any investments they make in new programs will yield positive results. Becoming a learning organization, or otherwise trying to transform your company through TQM or Business Process Reengineering, requires large investments of time, money, and other resources, investments that cannot be made casually or without having clear, measurable goals. Let's not fool ourselves—these are "bet-your-job" and sometimes "bet-your-company" investments.

As a result, before committing to the learning organization or any other transformation initiative, company managers rightfully ask some basic questions: What results can we expect? Will we reduce costs? Will we shorten time cycles for new product development? Will we reduce manpower needs? Basically, the questions boil down to "How will we know if we have succeeded?"

Measuring for results is a three-step process, with all three steps needed to ensure that the program's objectives are met.

- Step 1. Write measurable objectives.

- Step 2. Plan programs to achieve those objectives.

- Step 3. Determine and measure meaningful outcomes.

STEP I. WRITE MEASURABLE OBJECTIVES

If you state your program's objectives correctly, in measurable terms, then you are halfway to evaluating the program. Properly stated objectives have measurable results built in:

■ Product defects will be reduced by 50 percent within two years.

■ The new product development cycle will be shortened from thirty months to fifteen months within three years.

■ The average time to process a purchase order will decrease to five days within six months.

These are all well-written, measurable program objectives because they specify both the result to be achieved and a time frame for its achievement. The programs leading to these results can be measured objectively.

If you don't start with measurable objectives, you will never be able to measure the results.

■ We want to increase product quality.

■ We will shorten time to market.

■ We will reduce employee turnover.

■ Our customers will be more satisfied.

These all may sound like good goals, but unless you attach measures and dates to each objective, you will never know how far you have come or how much farther you have left to travel.

Writing sensible objectives for a transformation program is not a trivial exercise. The objectives must be challenging, but not so overwhelming that employees believe them impossible to achieve. They also must be supported by specific activities that will lead to their accomplishment.

STEP 2. PLAN PROGRAMS TO MEET YOUR OBJECTIVES

Jack Benny once managed a team of "Hollywood All-Stars" at a celebrity softball game. After the first three batters struck out, he quit. When asked why he was quitting, he replied, "I told them each to go up and get a hit. If they're not going to do what I say, what can I do but quit?"

To state an objective without providing means for achieving that objective doesn't make sense. In looking at the means to meet your objectives, you must take a comprehensive approach. The five foundations for the learning organization are the right place to start.

The Need for Strong Foundations

With any transformation effort, the five foundations must be solidly in place before you start building a superstructure of high-level technologies and methodologies. Asking people, for example, to change lifelong ways of working will not succeed without strong, visible leadership. Nor will the transformation attempt bear fruit if workers don't have the basic skills needed to use new technologies and methodologies. Employees who fear that adopting someone else's methods will hurt their own job appraisals, or who are strongly tied to their local procedures and standards, won't implement new ways of working. Managers who prize their power and control above all else will not expedite new ways of working.

The foundations need to be put in place before you can start building the superstructure. Start by assessing the presence and strength of the five foundations in your company. (Instruments for an initial assessment are contained in appendix A.) This assessment will indicate which foundations are present and how strong they are. This is important information. Your program objectives tell you where you want to end up. The assessments locate your starting point. The chapters on each of the foundations provide ideas on how to build or strengthen each foundation, and chapter 9 ("Breathing Life into the Learning Organization") provides a framework for starting your work.

Erecting the Superstructure

Once the foundations are secure, you can start building the super-structure of business practices, work methods, and supporting technologies needed to implement your transformation initiative. There are many approaches to each program available from a variety of vendors and consultants. Whichever approach you choose to take, the probability of its success is improved greatly by the presence of strong foundations.

The most important point to remember is that any transforma-tion initiative requires a comprehensive approach, starting with the five foundations. Even with the foundations in place, the implemen-tation of any new methodology must be preceded by learning and followed by coaching, reinforcement, and recognition.

Comprehensive Program Planning

If you are shopping for a new car, there is a wide variety of models, and an even wider variety of options, from which you can select. All models have a basic framework of chassis, drive train, interior and exterior. These are the car's foundations that provide for basic transportation. Depending on your preferences, you can select from many different options for convenience, style, comfort, performance, and so on. But after all the choices have been considered, you negotiate with the dealer to buy the *whole package*.

The same approach should be used in planning programs to achieve your desired transformation. You start with the five foundations and then select the approach you want to take (learning organization, TQM, Business Process Reengineering, and so forth). Within each of those alternatives, you have many options regarding specific tools, technologies, and methodologies. These choices can be made on the basis of cost, comfort, style, and other factors. But to end up with a successful program, you have to choose a complete package. Unconnected elements won't get you where you want to go. For example, effective teamwork won't happen unless:

■ Leadership stresses the importance of teamwork.

■ Team members have the basic skills necessary to do their own jobs as well as to work as part of a team.

■ Team members have removed their functional blinders to see the larger picture and are committed to optimizing the work of the team, rather than their individual functional goals.

■ The team is given an opportunity to develop its team skills, its cooperative work skills, and its management skills.

■ Managers of the individual team members are willing to support the team and to relinquish some of their authority to the team process.

■ Administrative systems support teamwork.

Comprehensive program planning means that your root problems must be diagnosed before you start to plan programs to solve them. Too often, companies spend large amounts of time and resources treating the symptoms, rather than the root problem, and never discover what the root problem really is. Hitting the right solution through this piecemeal approach depends on luck. Without luck, your fate may parallel that of the poor Indian chicken farmer described below.

A poor Indian chicken farmer had lived for many years outside Bombay, earning a meager living for his family with his chickens and their eggs. One morning, as he went out to feed his flock, he found several dead chickens. Not knowing what to do, he packed a bag and made the long trek into the Himalayas, climbed a high mountain, and found a guru.

"Oh, Guru!" he pleaded. "Some of my chickens are dead!"

"What do you feed them?" asked the guru.

"I give them wheat" was the answer.

"Corn!" instructed the guru. "Change their feed from wheat to corn and your problem will be solved."

The farmer thanked the guru and made the long trek back home. He changed the chickens' feed from wheat to corn and for three weeks, everything was fine. Then, one morning, he discovered more dead chickens. He packed his bag and again made the trek to the mountains to find the guru.

"Oh, Guru! More of my chickens are dead!"

"How do you give them water?" asked the guru.

"I give them water in wooden bowls that I carved myself," the farmer replied.

"Troughs! You must build water troughs!"

The farmer again thanked the guru, returned home and built troughs. For the next three months, everything was fine until, one morning, he found more dead chickens.

Returning to the mountain, he again addressed the guru: "Oh, Guru! More of my chickens have died!"

"How do you house your flock?" he asked.

"They live in a wooden chicken coop I built many years ago."

"Ventilation! They need more ventilation!"

Back home, the farmer spent every cent he could scrape up on a new ventilation system. For a year, his flock flourished. Then, one morning, he awoke to find ALL of the chickens dead. Sadly, he made a last trip to the guru.

"Oh, Guru!" he moaned. "All of my chickens are dead!"

"That's a shame," replied the guru. "I had a lot more solutions."

Taking a comprehensive approach to program planning mandates that you also take a comprehensive approach to program evaluation.

STEP 3. MEASURE MEANINGFUL OUTCOMES

When you buy a new car, you make your choice after considering many available models and options. When you subsequently are asked if you like your car, your answer probably will be based on your overall satisfaction, even though there may be some features that you dislike.

In the same vein, you need to evaluate your transformation initiative on the basis of the total program and the overall results. Having stated your objectives in measurable terms, you have ready-made measures of meaningful outcomes. Was your objective to "reduce the number of product defects by 50 percent within two years"? With measures of product defects at the start of the program, and then two years later, you can tell whether you have achieved your objective. You may also want to gather some interim measures periodically to report on ongoing progress toward the objective.

There are many types of measures that can be utilized, from

return on investment (ROI) to quality statistics to employee turn-over to customer satisfaction. The key to the overall program evaluation is to have stated the desired outcomes as part of the program's initial objectives. As I noted earlier, properly written objectives provide the program's evaluation measures.

Evaluating Piece Parts

In many situations, company managers insist that every program element be evaluated separately on the basis of return on invest-ment (ROI). The problem with this approach is that the various program elements are so interdependent that it is often impossible to measure the direct effects of a single component.

Motorola has stated that its return on its training investment is thirty to one. That is, for every dollar spent on training, there is a $30 increase in the trainees' productivity. Every training manager in the world would love to have a number like that to report to company management! And while I do not doubt the value and effectiveness of Motorola's training programs, I believe this is a very false and misleading number.

The real return to Motorola's investment in its transformation is probably less than thirty to one. This number is used because it was easy to derive—productivity increases versus the expenditure on training. But to achieve these productivity increases, Motorola invested in more than just training. It invested in the overall trans-formation effort, including changes in organizational design, man-agement practice, and the other foundations *in addition to* the investment in training programs on the superstructure, such as the use of quality tools. It is not so easy to measure how much Mo-torola invested in these other programs, so they use the easiest measure of investment—how much was spent on training.

Motorola's high return on its training investment would not be possible unless the company had built strong foundations of organizational design, management practice, and leadership. Another company, using the identical Motorola training curriculum, may show no return on its training investment. The reason? Managers at the other company may not allow their employees to use what they have learned; that is, employees may receive data and information through training programs, but will not be allowed to apply that information to their jobs—to transform the information into knowledge. The training programs in this company are not supported by the same foundations that exist in Motorola and, as a result, won't reap the same returns on the identical investment in training.

If the measurement of investments and returns is so difficult, how do you evaluate the piece parts? How do you choose among the cloth, fabric, and leather interiors? How do you examine each element in the full range of learning activities to determine whether they should be part of the overall package? The three key measures are:

- Relevance.
- Value.
- Quality.

Relevance

Whether the change involves a training program, a new piece of personal computer software, or a new job description, the employees being affected must consider the changes *relevant* to what they are doing. New data will remain only data, and will not be retained, unless they are relevant to people's work. If people do not consider something relevant to what they are doing, they will not bother learning.

- In an earlier example, salespeople considered data on a new product line irrelevant because they were not being goaled on selling those products.

- A group of people who were sent to a team-building program considered it irrelevant because they never considered themselves part of a team.

- A new spreadsheet program installed on all of the company's computer systems is irrelevant to people who have been doing all of their work satisfactorily on a different spreadsheet.

To make any of these changes relevant, the employees' context must be changed. Changing context is not accomplished through training or new work tools—it is the job of company leadership to provide a new context that will make these tools and methods relevant to their employees.

- Sales management can add the new product line to the sales goal sheets, thereby making it relevant to the sales efforts.

- The group manager can explain why her employees need to start working more as a team and change job measurements to reflect the value she is placing on teamwork.

- The company's vice president of finance can explain that the company needs to settle on a single spreadsheet program to be used across all financial departments to allow for easier exchange of information.

All of these actions by managers make the changes relevant to the employees being affected. Once the employees recognize the relevance of the changes to their work, they will be more receptive to them and will work to take the new data and transform them into useful information and knowledge.

Value

Assuming that employees find the new training program, work methods, or tools relevant, they must also perceive that they *add value* to what they are doing and are being measured on.

- The new product line may appear on a salesperson's goal sheet, but unless he sees how it adds value, he still won't sell it, preferring to sell other products or services with which both he and his customers are more familiar. Only if he sees that the new product line can make his sales efforts more successful—it opens, for example, new sales opportunities or gives him a new competitive advantage against the company's major rival—will he actively sell the new products.

- The department's employees, if they are to adopt team-related work methods, must view teamwork as a way of making their jobs easier or making them more effective in their work. Unless they perceive the value added by teamwork, no amount of training will get them to work as a team.

- The finance people who are used to doing their jobs with a different spreadsheet will not welcome the new corporate standard unless they see advantages for themselves. Will they now be able to electronically import data that they previously had to enter manually because of system incompatibility? Will they now be able to use a standard set of electronic report formats instead of manually extracting and typing their weekly reports? These types of changes add value to their work and make it much more likely that they will accept the new system.

When looking at the value added by these types of changes, you must also look at the negatives to ensure that the incremental value exceeds the perceived negatives. For example:

- Salespeople may find the new product line too complicated to understand. Rather than look foolish trying to explain it to customers, they may avoid selling it.

- The new team members may feel that they no longer have a way of demonstrating their individual excellence and may worry that their future salary increases may be compromised if credit for their work is shared by other team members.

- Individual members of the finance department may have felt powerful when they controlled their own data—people had to come to them to get access to it. The new company standard, where all spreadsheets can now be commonly accessed, may lessen this "power."

Once you have determined that your planned approach is both relevant and adds value, you now need to focus on the quality of the program.

Quality

The third measure for the individual parts of your overall program plan is *quality*. Too often, companies are so focused on the quality issue with respect to their external customers that they ignore quality considerations in developing programs for their own employees.

Most training and development evaluation handbooks present a wide variety of quality measures for training efforts. For example:

- Were the slides or other visual aids clear and understandable?

- Was the classroom comfortable?

- Did the instructor allow time for, and answer, student questions?

- Were student materials well written?
  . . . and dozens of other measures.

The problem with a lot of these quality measures is that they can all be met and still provide a poor program. That is why I believe that the first two quality measures must be relevance and value. When it comes to the quality of the actual delivery of the program, there are three basic criteria that should be used:

- Were the goals of the program clear, and did it meet those goals? Too often, whether in a formal classroom, in a coaching session with a manager, or in other "learning" circumstances, the participants aren't sure why they are there or what is supposed to be happening. Learning, in any setting, will not occur unless the participants know what is expected of them and the program elements are tied to those expectations.

- Was the "provider" knowledgeable and did she meet the needs of the participants? A "provider" can be an instructor in a formal classroom setting, a manager providing one-on-one coaching to an employee, or a presenter at a meeting. Whoever the person, and whatever the setting, the provider must know what he is talking about and present it in a way that makes sense to the learners.

- Did the surroundings and materials facilitate learning? Whether in a classroom, a manager's office, or a conference room, the environmental conditions should not distract the learning process. Similarly, any learning materials (presentation materials, texts, tools, and machines) must contribute to the learning process.

Certainly, it is nice to have state-of-the-art classrooms and laboratories, professionally developed media, and four-color instructional manuals that win industry awards. But an effective learning environment depends more on the people involved than on any fancy material and luxurious setting. Quality is a measure of the skills, knowledge, and abilities of the people involved in the learning effort.

MEASURING *ALL* OF THE RESULTS

Your main purpose in building a learning organization may be to reduce time to market, to reduce levels of management, or to improve customer satisfaction. But along with this major purpose will come many additional benefits, such as:

- Increased employee loyalty and reduced turnover.

- Greater individual and organizational productivity.

- A new esprit de corps at all levels of the organization.

- A raft of ideas for new products and services.

Some of these are easier to quantify than others. The important point here is that these other benefits of your transformation effort should also be taken into account in measuring the results of your program efforts. Companies such as Motorola, Corning, General Electric, which are the subject of endless articles about their successful transformations, certainly get some business benefit from all that good press.

> Gordon Lankton, CEO of NYPRO, told me, "When we have customers come through our plant, and we get a lot of them, they usually end up in my office at the end of the day. They used to make remarks about the nice job we did refurbishing the old mill building or about how clean our manufacturing plant is. Now, all they talk about is training—how impressed they are with all we are doing with the NYPRO Institute." Lankton can't put a dollar value on these remarks, but he is certain that customer impressions about the excellence of his company's training efforts are worth a lot of real business.

KEY POINTS

Measuring for results starts with the definition of quantifiable objectives. When properly stated, the objectives of your transformation initiative will provide their own evaluation measures. It is important that when planning your initiative, you take a comprehensive view of all the changes in policies, procedures, business practices, work methods, and so forth, needed to make the transformation work.

The comprehensive package is what needs to be measured. Evaluation of the piece parts should also be done, but only to ensure that they are contributing to the effort. It is very difficult, and I would argue not very wise, to try to justify each separate program element on the basis of ROI. Instead, you should be measuring each on the basis of its relevance to the program goals, the value it adds, and the quality of the effort.

Also remember that in addition to your stated goals for the

transformation initiative, there will certainly be a set of added benefits that also should be taken into account in evaluating your overall results. Employee satisfaction, reduced turnover, increased creativity, and other factors are sometimes difficult to measure in dollar terms, but they certainly add value to your program efforts.

TWELVE

NURTURING LEARNING BEYOND THE NEXT QUARTER

Learning never stops. Just as competitors, customers, and technologies constantly change, so companies must continually learn in order to keep up and get ahead. The learning organization is never frozen. There will never be a time when a company can say, "We have the perfect organization, optimal work methods, and the perfect set of products and services. We can stop now and be assured of a prosperous future." The revolution must continue. The five foundations for the learning organization are the basis of the revolution.

One of the hallmarks of the TQM movement is continuous improvement. Continuous improvement does not have a time horizon—neither does organizational learning. Continuous learning is a prerequisite to continuous improvement: acquiring new information, and transforming that information into knowledge through application on the job, is what makes continuous improvement possible.

Breakthroughs, those quantum leaps in productivity, time reductions, and quality, can happen at any time, but are most likely to occur in the first stages of building the learning organization. But improvement never stops. The 1 and 2 and 5 percent improvements will be continuous as people learn more about their work and how it fits into the company's overall business, as they apply their knowledge, and the wisdom they acquire through experience, to finding ever-better ways of getting their jobs done.

The "learning revolution" is indeed a revolution, requiring massive upheavals in the status quo. It requires strong leadership, gut-wrenching changes, and the forbearance to withstand a lot of pain. Not everyone in the company will survive. Noel Tichy, writing about General Electric's revolution, says:

> Replacing the old way with the new does not happen at the touch of a button. It requires deep convictions, enormous upheavals, a vision of what lies ahead, and perseverance even when the pain seems unbearable. But the ultimate benefits—for stockholders and employees alike—are enormous.[1]

If you are willing to make this commitment, start with the five foundations. Once the foundations are in place, you can then move on to erecting the superstructure—the higher-level skills and methods of the learning organization.

THE SUPERSTRUCTURE OF THE LEARNING ORGANIZATION

The superstructure of the learning organization has three major components that together enable people within the company to continually create new knowledge assets, the key to long-term survival and competitive advantage. These are:

- Continuous inquiry.

- Information capture.

- Information dissemination.

We'll examine each separately and then see how they work together in the learning organization.

CONTINUOUS INQUIRY

In the learning organization, people are continually seeking a better understanding of their customers' needs and their own business processes and work methods. At the same time, they try to better understand the company's products and services and determine how they can be improved. Together, all of these elements provide the information necessary to plan all parts of the company's future, from its products and services to its markets to the structure of its complete internal and external value chains.

Understanding the Customer

The customer is where it all begins. Without understanding the customer's needs, a company cannot succeed. Strong customer relationships can yield information related to:

- Product and service quality.

- New ways of using the company's products and services that can lead to new customers and market niches.

- Ideas for future products and services.

A lot of lip service has been paid to forming strong customer relationships over the years. But in many companies, salespeople are so pressured to make the next sale that they never have enough time to develop the relationship. In the learning organization, customers are viewed as an important link in the company's value chain and as an invaluable source of learning. No new product or service is ever developed without solid customer input.

Understanding Business Processes

Business processes in the learning organization are thoroughly understood by everyone involved. Process modeling, begun in the building of the third foundation, "overcoming functional myopia," enables all parties to the process to understand how their individual tasks relate to the overall work of the company. With this understanding, employees can modify or reengineer a process to improve both efficiency and effectiveness, getting rid of those parts of the process that do not add value.

But business processes change over time. As people learn from experience, adopt new work methods, and introduce new technologies, they will find even better ways of accomplishing their work. Business processes must be continually examined and must be open to continuous improvement.

A company's internal business processes are also very reliant on the business processes of its suppliers and customers. So, while starting with internal business processes, the learning organization extends its analysis and reengineering efforts to include links throughout its value chain. The need for continuous improvement similarly extends throughout the value chain, meaning that customers and suppliers may suggest modifications of their own or the company's processes to improve the overall efficiency of the complete chain.

In the learning organization, no existing business process, no work method, is sacrosanct—everything is open to constant inquiry, as well as continual learning and improvement. The methods needed to do this include process analysis and reengineering, as discussed earlier, as well as systematic problem solving and experimentation.

Systematic Problem Solving

The steps of the scientific method for problem solving are well established and are taught in many seminars around the world. It starts with problem identification, analysis, the generation and evaluation of alternative solutions, selection of one solution, implementation, and evaluation. But these methods are often given more lip service than application in the real world of business.

■ Understanding the Problem

Too often, we are so alarmed by a problem situation that we rush to fix it without ever understanding what the real problem is. The result is a system so full of patches, baling wire, and chewing gum that while hasty solutions keep it going, everyone knows that one day it will all blow up.

> A senior engineering manager was called to a meeting of the company's executive committee. The CEO asked him to take on a new assignment. "We have six different groups working on different solutions to our new product set. They don't talk to each other and are working at cross-purposes. We want you to put together a team to determine exactly what we should be doing with these products and how best we can get the products to market within the next eighteen months. Start right now and come back to this meeting in two weeks with a solution."
>
> Two weeks later, the engineering manager returned. "What's your solution?" asked the CEO.

"I've spent the past two weeks getting a full understanding of the problem," replied the engineering manager. "Let me spend the next half-hour explaining the problem to you, so that we can all start from the same place."

"That's not what we asked you to do!" shouted the CEO. "You were supposed to have some solutions to report to us today!"

"Solutions to what?" asserted the manager. "If I started out trying to come up with a solution, as you requested, I'd probably come up with a great solution—to the wrong problem. If you'll indulge me so that we can all agree on the exact nature of the problem, I'll come back next week with a solution that I'll guarantee you will work in the time frame you've requested."

The CEO and the executive committee concurred, the problem was agreed upon, and the manager came back the next week with a solution to the problem. Later in the day, the CEO called the manager and told him that he had done the right thing.

Systematic problem solving requires more than just learning the techniques of the scientific method, it also requires:

- The discipline to apply the problem-solving methods correctly, and not jump to hasty, and often incorrect or partially correct, solutions.

- The support of top management to question the status quo, to break the old rules if required to come up with the right solution. (How many good ideas are killed with comments like "That's not the way we do things here" or "That may work in the laboratory, but the politics in this organization will never let it happen here in the real world"?)

- The time to do it right.

In many companies, problems arise so constantly, and the pressure to solve them is so great, that no one ever has the time or discipline to really apply the scientific method. These companies are stuck in what I call the "Firefighter Syndrome."

The Firefighter Syndrome

Many managers complain: "The fires never stop. I don't know how much more of this my people and I can take—it's just one fire after another. We never have time to get any real work done."

When someone suggests to these managers that perhaps they ought to take time to do some planning, that there may be a way to prevent future fires so that their groups can get back to their "real work," they typically reply, "I wish we had the time, but we don't. We've got to put out those fires or we'll all lose our heads."

Many companies give out "Firefighter of the Week [Month/Year]" awards to employees who have come to the rescue in a problem situation. While heroics may be of value in specific situations, these companies would be better served by giving awards for fire prevention. If a manager finds that his department is spending a great proportion of its time fighting fires, he should realize that something is very wrong.

Many years ago, I spent a summer working for the mayor of a small city. Two other graduate students and I were to test the feasibility of instituting a "program budgeting" system for the city.

One of the departments I worked with was the city's fire department. In a meeting with the fire chief and his two deputies, I started discussing performance measures for the department. "What proportion of your time would you say the department spends fighting fires?" I asked. I knew it would be a relatively small number. When they were reluctant to answer the question, I suggested, "Would you say five percent?"

The chief looked at me and replied, "If we spent five percent of our time actually fighting fires, this entire city would be in ashes. The number is probably more like one percent, two percent tops."

The point the chief made was that the people's confidence in the fire department came not from knowing they put out X fires yesterday, but from knowing that the fire department was *ready* to help them in an emergency.

The fire department's major work is in fire prevention and in being ready to respond to emergencies. Its preparation comes from studying the city and the businesses within the city to understand how they are structured, how they work, what materials they use, and so forth. The department also spends a lot of time studying the science of fire, rescue methods, and emergency medical procedures to understand how best to fight various types of fires and respond to other emergency situations.

The parallel for the business manager is to develop a thorough understanding of her company's business processes and methods. This can best be done through the use of process modeling and value chain analysis methods. When the total process is understood, the manager can then select the optimal methods for her own group's work in order to provide maximum added value and to prevent fires from happening in the first place. The key to solving any problem is to first understand it.

By instituting systematic problem solving, by creating the discipline within all employees to stick with the methodology, you move from firefighting mode to fire prevention. This is not to say that fires will never occur in the learning organization, but only that fires will become much less frequent and your employees will be much better prepared to fight them when they do occur. One way of evaluating potential solutions to a problem is through careful experimentation.

Experimentation

The "perfect" solution to a problem is not always obvious, and what we consider today's perfect solution may be replaced with an even better one tomorrow. The learning organization constantly experiments with new ways of doing its work, always seeking that next plateau.

Does this mean that everyone in the learning organization is forever changing the ways they work? No, for this would result in chaos—no one would ever be able to rely on her knowledge of how the overall process works. Experimentation must occur, but it must be systematic and controlled. There are two preconditions to successful experimentation:

- An environment that nurtures experimentation and risk taking.

- Employees who know how to design, conduct, and evaluate experiments.

■ The Right Environment

Not all experiments yield positive results—many don't work. (If they all worked, they wouldn't be "experiments.") Employees who fear that an unsuccessful experiment will lead to punishment (loss of job, poor performance rating) will not experiment. The environment of the learning organization encourages experimentation and rewards people for conducting thoughtful, well-designed experiments.

Experimentation is just another learning method. It stretches people's knowledge and tests their wisdom. Edison tested thousands of materials that couldn't be used for electric lightbulb filaments before he found one that could. If there is no experimentation, learning will be limited to what is already known. And today's knowledge, in a world of instantaneous communications, cannot provide competitive advantage. The creation of new knowledge is what gives companies the edge in the marketplace, and experimentation creates new knowledge.

■ A Disciplined Approach to Experimentation

Designing experiments is itself a science. It starts with an understanding of the status quo, that is, a thorough understanding of current business processes and work methods. Without a model of the current state, you won't be able to tell if anything has changed or if the results come from the experiment or somewhere else. Experiments typically are limited to changing one or a few variables in the process—if too many experiments are being done simultaneously on the same business process, it will be difficult or impossible to determine which variable caused which result.

To experiment properly, employees need training in the scientific method and must develop a thorough understanding of the methods and processes with which they are experimenting. They must also be given the time and tools to conduct proper experiments so that the company can have confidence in the results.

INFORMATION CAPTURE

Learning involves capturing information and transforming that information into knowledge through application on the job. In the learning organization, people capture information from a variety of sources, including:

- Past experience.

- The experiences of other companies.

- Research results, theory, and other information available in the public domain.

Learning from Past Experience

There is important information to be derived from both successful and failed experiments, projects, and programs. Too often, this information is not collected or, if collected, it sits in file cabinets and on bookshelves. Information that is not used has no value. The result is that others in the company will make the same mistakes, or miss opportunities for improvement, simply because they "didn't know."

In the learning organization, information from others' work, both successes and failures, is captured and made available to anyone who needs it. This can be done in a number of ways. Harvard Business School professor David Garvin reports several examples:

- Boeing created Project Homework to "compare the development processes of the 737 and 747 with those of the 707 and 727, two of the company's most profitable planes."[2] The result was an inch-thick notebook full of lessons learned.

- Paul Revere Life Insurance "requires all problem-solving teams to complete short registration forms describing their proposed projects. . . . The company then enters the forms into its computer system and can immediately retrieve a listing of other groups of people who have worked or are working on the topic."[3]

Earlier cited examples of this type of learning from past experience include:

- NYPRO Plastics annual meetings of plant managers from around the world to share experiences, successes, and problems.

- Xerox's institutionalizing the "folklore" of service technicians' experiences.

Another example comes from Digital Equipment Corporation. Using network-based computer conferences, a salesperson might seek guidance on a customer request, such as: "My customer has the following configuration of non-Digital equipment and the following Digital equipment [detailed lists follow in the message]. The customer wants to integrate everything into a single network. He has heard of a third-party product called [name deleted]. Does anyone have experience with a similar situation?" Within a day of entering this query into the conference, the salesperson will likely get several responses. For example:

- "I had a similar customer situation, and they decided to use the same third-party product. They had some problems with it. But if you [instructions provided], it should work well."

- "My customer found another third-party product [name and contact provided] that worked much better than the product your customer is asking about."

- "We did a custom integration project for a customer with a very similar situation. Call me at [number] and we can discuss making it available to your customer."

These responses likely come from people unknown to the person making the query, sometimes in the same city, sometimes from across the globe. Preserving the organization's memory and history can help to avoid many costly errors and lost opportunities.

Learning from Others

Not all knowledge exists within any given organization. There is much to be learned from others. "Others" include people from outside your own function or organization, but still inside your company, as well as from those outside the company. This type of learning requires a solid footing on the foundation of "overcoming functional myopia"—companies that suffer from the not-invented-here (NIH) syndrome will not allow learning from others.

There are many ways in which individuals, teams, functions, and whole companies can learn from others:

- The most popular term for learning from others is "benchmarking." This is a formal approach to identifying the best practitioners in other companies, systematically studying their practices, and then adapting them for your own company.

- General Electric does a lot of internal benchmarking. Under a program called "Best Practices," GE had a team of top-level managers study best practices in all of GE's operations worldwide and work to get them adopted by other GE units.

- Reading industry and trade journals, attending trade shows and public symposia, keep employees aware of what others are doing and give them ideas for how to improve their own companies' practices.

- Studying how customers use the company's products and services, and discussing their operations with them, will also yield ideas for new products and services or give clues as to how current products and services can be improved.

As David Garvin says, "Learning organizations . . . cultivate the art of open, attentive listening."[4]

Information from the Public Domain

In the learning organization, people also keep up-to-date on information available in the public domain. This includes review of industry and professional publications, academic journals, newspapers and newsletters, and listening to consultants and vendors who have created new business approaches. It also includes attending professional society conferences and academic symposia and getting on university mailing lists for "working papers" that they publish. Learning organizations are constantly on the watch for new ideas and new methods that may help them improve their own performance.

INFORMATION DISSEMINATION

The key to the learning organization is ensuring that people have access to the information they need when they need it. The information necessary to fix a problem or create a new opportunity may exist within a company, but it is worthless unless it is accessible by the people who have those responsibilities. Companies waste millions of dollars, countless hours, and many other resources trying to find answers that already exist. The transfer of information— making it widely available and accessible—is what helps companies avoid these costs.

There are many methods of spreading information that have already been discussed throughout this book, ranging from formal training programs to computer-based conferences to informal discussions with others inside and across organizational and company bounds. But information transfer can only occur if:

- You know where the information resides.

- Those holding the information are willing to share it.

- Those needing the information are willing to learn from others.

Knowing Where Information Resides

Many companies have developed elaborate systems that enable them to locate a part no matter where it resides in the company. Companies need to develop similar systems to keep track of their inventories of information and skills. This type of system would keep track of project and program information, the skills and experiences of employees, and libraries of internal and external data related to the company's business processes, work methods, products, and services. The system developed by Paul Revere Life Insurance, cited earlier, is the start of such a system.

These systems must be accessible to all company employees. When teaching grade-school students to use a dictionary, teachers typically tell them that "knowing how to find the answer is just as important as knowing the answer." Unless the people who need the information have some way of locating it, it may as well not exist at all.

Willingness to Share Information

One of the most frequently cited reasons why middle managers often become barriers to transformation efforts is that they know a key fact: "Knowledge is power." Many employees have been guilty of hoarding information because it makes them feel powerful. It also provides job security: "They can't get rid of me, I know too much that no one else knows."

Even if it isn't a matter of hoarding information for power

purposes, many people are reluctant to share information, feeling that it will take too much time away from their "real work." When I started Digital's Network University, many engineers were very reluctant to participate in the program. They knew that they had important information that the program participants wanted, but felt that it wasn't their job to be doing instruction.

In the learning organization, the sharing of information becomes a performance measure—people are rewarded for sharing information, for spreading their knowledge to others. If people aren't willing to share information, learning cannot take place.

Willingness to Learn

The learning organization requires that the individual be willing to learn from others. Individuals and groups have to realize that the ways in which they work, no matter how successful they have been, can always be improved.

Part of the problem is that some individuals are elitist in their attitudes toward learning. When engineers at Digital Equipment Corporation started acting as instructors in the Network University program, they quickly discovered that the salespeople who were their students had a lot of valuable information. For most of these engineers, this was a revelation—salespeople were considerably "below" engineers in the Digital pecking order. Engineers learned from professors and more senior engineers—not from mere salespeople! But once the first few engineers saw the value in these learning interactions, and reported them to their colleagues, they all became anxious to participate in the next program.

In the learning organization, people are respected for their knowledge and the information they can share, no matter their function or level. Engineers can learn from salespeople, managers from their employees, executives from customers.

KEY POINTS

The development of a learning organization is not something you do this quarter and then return to business as usual. The learning organization is a vital, dynamic organism that must be sustained over time.

After building solid foundations for the learning organization, you can start erecting the superstructure. This superstructure consists of methodologies, technologies, and business practices that encourage:

- Continuous inquiry—the constant search for ever-better ways of accomplishing individual and organizational goals.

- Information capture—capturing all available information from any and all internal and external sources, as well as creating new knowledge through controlled experimentation.

- Information dissemination—ensuring that the people who need any given piece of information have access to it and know how to go about capturing it for themselves.

AFTERWORD

The fully implemented learning organization results in a dynamic, energized company environment where all employees at all levels look forward to coming to work each day. Employees know that each day will be different from the last, that the challenge of today is to build on what they have already created for themselves and for their fellow employees. Visitors to the learning organization feel an energy buzzing through the offices and factories. Customers look forward to their interactions with company personnel. Suppliers value their relationships with the company and emulate them with their other customers and their own suppliers.

> I first visited NYPRO in 1979 while working at a local community college. Then a very small plastics manufacturer, the company had done a remarkable job in converting an old New England textile mill to a modern manufacturing plant. Even then, you could feel an energy among employees who were molding plastic parts for small hair dryers and assembling the finished product for NYPRO's customer, Gillette.
>
> As I started doing research for this book, people from

many different sources told me that I should visit NYPRO, that they had been very impressed with presentations they had seen by NYPRO personnel and continually heard good things about what was happening at the company.

When I visited again in early 1993, the atmosphere was even more exciting than I had remembered. Now one of twenty NYPRO plants and joint ventures around the world, the Clinton, Massachusetts, plant had grown to encompass additional buildings in the mill complex. The NYPRO Institute had added several modern classrooms and lab facilities, serving not only NYPRO employees but also their families, local high school students, customers, and suppliers.

I expected that Paul Jensen, the director of the NYPRO Institute, would be very proud and enthusiastic about all that he had accomplished. But I had rarely seen this type of enthusiasm for a company's training activities mirrored in its top business executives. Brian Jones, president of the Clinton plant, talked proudly, not only of the institute and its programs, but also of the excellence of his own staff of managers who guided their employees' and their own learning activities.

Similarly, CEO Gordon Lankton views the institute as the company's shining star, at the same time emphasizing the responsibility of all company managers around the globe for fostering their employees' learning. He points with pride to the display of awards made to the company by its customers worldwide. These customers have sought out NYPRO, even when there have been ample numbers of more local suppliers who could have met their needs.

The learning organization focuses on harnessing not only the company's potential, but also that of each individual employee. It recognizes that its only sustainable competitive advantage comes from its knowledge assets, and that those assets are embodied in its employees. The learning organization ensures its future success because, rather than waiting for external factors to determine its directions, it creates its own future.

> Digital Equipment Corporation's Network University, was a remarkable learning program. The esprit de corps, spanning the entire Digital networks world, and the excitement of the semi-annual programs were exhilarating. Network University was an ongoing experiment in learning methods. It was unlike anything that Digital had ever done before and, to the best of my knowledge, unlike any other industry program.
>
> Being an experiment, not everything worked always. But the enthusiasm of the audience for the efforts of all involved in producing these large events gave everyone a positive attitude, even when something went awry.
>
> First-time attendees at a Network University session got immediately caught up in the energy of the people. Network University was a grueling event, starting with a dinner on Sunday evening and continuing ten to fourteen hours a day for the rest of the week. But enthusiasm overcame exhaustion, for the participants knew that every one of the hundreds of people there were unparalleled learning resources, all dedicated to helping each other and the company succeed in the networks business.
>
> For all of the high-ranking Digital managers who attended Network University, we kept the focus on the real stars—the sales and sales support people who were actually making it all work for the company. This point was best made in August 1987, when we had our largest single session, with nine hundred participants. Rather than introducing Bob Murray, the manager of Networks and Communications Marketing, who sponsored the event, and Bill Johnson, Digital's vice president for networks and communications, I simply called them up to the front of the hotel

ballroom and said, "Bill and Bob—I'd like to introduce to you the people from Digital's worldwide field organization who in the past twelve months broke the billion-dollar mark in networking sales."

You, too, can create your own learning organization. You can develop an environment where your employees look forward to each day's challenges, where learning and improvement grow, hand in hand, to create extraordinary business results. You can look forward to each new business day—not fearing the fires that will spring up today—and to continuous improvement and breakthroughs that delight not only your own employees, but also your customers and everyone else they work with throughout your company's value chain.

Becoming a learning organization is not dependent on the business your company is in. Manufacturing, services—any company in any industry can benefit from this transformation. But the learning organization, or any other corporate transformation effort, can only be successful if it is built upon a set of solid foundations. The types of changes in culture and business practice implied by these efforts are difficult and will create shock waves throughout the organization. Without solid foundations, these shocks can be enough to bring down the mightiest of companies. The five foundations for the learning organization provide a solid basis for the re-education of the corporation and the establishment of the superstructure needed to complete your transformation and ensure your future success.

APPENDIX A

FINDING YOUR STARTING POINT

To find your starting point for developing a learning organization, you must assess the presence and strength of your five foundations. The questions listed below should help you make these assessments. If the answers to all or most of the questions for each foundation are "No," you will need to start building that foundation from scratch. If the answers to several of the questions are "Yes," the foundation is present, but may need some strengthening.

FOUNDATION I: VISIBLE LEADERSHIP

1. We have a well-defined, easily understood   Yes   No
   vision for the entire company.
2. There is total agreement on the vision   Yes   No
   across all levels, functions, and divisions.
3. All company leaders are committed to the   Yes   No
   transformation effort and are committed
   to seeing it through.

4. Company management has developed   Yes   No
   thorough plans to implement the
   transformation program and has
   committed sufficient resources to ensure
   the plan's success.

5. The transformation program spans *all*   Yes   No
   parts of the company, with no group
   being exempt.

FOUNDATION 2: "THINKING" LITERACY

6. The company has identified the sets of   Yes   No
   basic skills needed for all jobs within the
   company.

7. The company has assessed the basic skills   Yes   No
   levels of all employees to determine
   training needs.

8. The company sponsors needed remedial   Yes   No
   basic skills instruction for all employees,
   either in-house or in cooperation with
   local educational agencies.

9. The company encourages all employees   Yes   No
   to exceed basic skills requirements and
   provides opportunities for such
   education, either on-site or by paying
   employees' tuition at local schools and
   colleges.

10. The company invests in basic business,   Yes   No
    team, communication, and self-
    management skills training (in addition
    to the three Rs) for all employees.

FOUNDATION 3: OVERCOMING FUNCTIONAL MYOPIA

11.	All company business processes have been charted and analyzed.	Yes	No
12.	All employees understand the company's basic value chain and how their work fits into that chain.	Yes	No
13.	Cross-functional teamwork is common practice.	Yes	No
14.	Employees are measured not only by functional goals and standards, but also by how much they contribute to the overall success of the company.	Yes	No
15.	Administrative politicies and procedures encourage a wide view of the company's business.	Yes	No

FOUNDATION 4: EFFECTIVE LEARNING TEAMS

16.	Teamwork is viewed as a common way of working, rather than as an exception to normal work practices.	Yes	No
17.	Measurement and reward systems recognize the value of teamwork and not just of individual achievement.	Yes	No
18.	The company has a comprehensive plan for team development, including formal training programs and ongoing coaching.	Yes	No
19.	Empowered, self-managed teams are eliminating the need for some managers.	Yes	No
20.	Teamwork has resulted in significant business results, such as, reduction in time, costs, or defects.	Yes	No

FOUNDATION 5: MANAGERS AS ENABLERS

21. The company has redefined middle management jobs, making middle managers more responsible for the development of their employees.   Yes   No

22. The company provides training and development programs to help middle managers learn new skills, such as coaching.   Yes   No

23. Managers view their new roles as teacher, team builder, and coach positively.   Yes   No

24. Managers are viewed by employees as champions of new work methods, rather than as obstacles to them.   Yes   No

25. The company has provided new opportunities for many displaced managers, rather than just showing them the door.   Yes   No

GUIDE TO
ADDITIONAL RESOURCES

LEARNING ORGANIZATIONS

The one book most responsible for popularizing the term "the learning organization" is Peter Senge's *The Fifth Discipline: The Art and Practice of the Learning Organization* (New York: Doubleday/Currency, 1990). Other authors who have written about the learning organization include:

- Chris Argyris, *Knowledge for Action* (San Francisco: Jossey-Bass, 1993).

- Charles Handy, *The Age of Unreason* (Boston: Harvard Business School Press, 1991).

Harvard Business School professor David Garvin had an excellent article, "Building a Learning Organization" in the July–August 1993 issue of *Harvard Business Review*.

One other book stands out on the subject of individual learning within organizations:

- Calhoun W. Wick and Lu Stanton Leon, *The Learning Edge* (New York: McGraw-Hill, 1993).

LEADERSHIP

There are dozens of books on leadership available. Several that I have found particularly helpful are:

- Edgar H. Schein, *Organizational Culture and Leadership*, 2d ed. (San Francisco: Jossey-Bass, 1992).

- Burt Nanus, *Visionary Leadership* (San Francisco: Jossey-Bass, 1992).

- Jay A. Conger, *Learning to Lead* (San Francisco: Jossey-Bass, 1992).

"THINKING" LITERACY

The most comprehensive treatment I have found of the skills needed by today's and tomorrow's worker is:

- Anthony P. Carnevale, Leila J. Gainer, and Ann S. Meltzer, *Workplace Basics* (San Francisco: Jossey-Bass, 1990). They also have as a companion volume a workbook on planning your own company's programs around workplace basics.

Two other books that also have interesting perspectives on these issues are:

- Stephen Brookfield, *Developing Critical Thinkers* (Bristol, PA: Taylor & Francis, 1987).

- Arthur G. Wirth, *Education and Work for the Year Two Thousand* (San Francisco: Jossey-Bass, 1992).

OVERCOMING FUNCTIONAL MYOPIA

Resources in this area deal with process reengineering and organizational architecture.

- Michael Hammer and James Champy, *Reengineering the Corporation* (New York: Harper Business, 1993).

- Jay R. Galbraith and Edward E. Lawler III, *Organizing for the Future* (San Francisco: Jossey-Bass, 1993).

- Dave Ulrich and Dale Lake, *Organizational Capability* (New York: Wiley, 1990).

- Donna R. Neusch and Alan F. Siebenaler, *The High Performance Enterprise* (Essex Junction, VT: The Oliver Wight Companies, 1993).

- Thomas H. Davenport, *Process Innovation* (Boston: Harvard Business School Press, 1993).

EFFECTIVE LEARNING TEAMS

Of the hundreds of books on teams and team building on the market, I found these particularly helpful:

- Peter R. Schultes, *The Team Handbook* (Madison, WI: Joiner Associates, 1988).

- Richard S. Wellins, William C. Byham, and Jeanne M. Wilson, *Empowered Teams* (San Francisco: Jossey-Bass, 1991).

- Jessica P. Lipnack and Jeffrey S. Stamps, *The TeamNet Factor* (Essex Junction, VT: The Oliver Wight Companies, 1993).

MANAGERS AS ENABLERS

The one management book that I have found most helpful in my own career is:

- David L. Bradford and Allan R. Cohen, *Managing for Excellence* (New York: Wiley, 1984).

Another book that deals directly with the role of manager as coach for self-directed work teams is:

- Kimball Fisher, *Leading Self-Directed Work Teams* (New York: McGraw-Hill, 1992).

TRAINING ORGANIZATIONS

The best overview of the state of training and development in American industry is:

- Anthony P. Carnevale, Leile J. Gainer, and Janice Villet, *Training in America* (San Francisco: Jossey-Bass, 1990).

To keep abreast of current issues and practices in the field, I would also recommend reading:

- *Training & Development*, a monthly publication of the American Society for Training & Development.

- *Training* magazine, a monthly publication of Lakewood Publications.

- *HR Magazine*, a monthly publication of the Society for Human Resource Management.

REFERENCES

Chapter 1. Foundations for the Learning Organization

1. "The REAL Economy," *The Atlantic Monthly*, February 1991, p. 42.
2. "Manage Change—Not the Chaos Caused By Change," by Beverly Goldberg, *Management Review*, November 1992, p. 40.
3. *Second to None*, Homewood, IL: Business One Irwin, 1992, p. 78.
4. "The Cost of Quality," *Newsweek*, September 7, 1992, p. 49.
5. Robert Chapman Wood, "A Hero without a Company," *Forbes*, March 18, 1991, pp. 112–114.
6. *Ibid.*
7. Richard Tanner Pascale, *Managing on the Edge*, New York: Simon & Schuster, 1990, p. 13.
8. "Jack Welch's Lessons for Success," *Fortune*, January 25, 1993, p. 88.
9. "Companies That Train Best," by Ronald Henkoff, *Fortune*, March 22, 1993, p. 62.
10. "Lifelong Learning for Economic Survival," Draft report, January 1993.
11. Speech to the M.I.T. Conference on Transforming Organizations, May 30, 1990.

Chapter 2. Leading the Revolution with Visible Leadership

1. Richard J. Schonberger, *World Class Manufacturing,* New York: The Free Press, 1986. It should be noted that at the time of Schonberger's book, Blount Canada Ltd. was known as Omark Industries.
2. Quoted by Noel M. Tichy and Stratford Sherman in *Control Your Destiny or Someone Else Will,* New York: Currency-Doubleday, 1993, pp. 329–340.
3. Quoted in "Leading the Way into the 21st Century," *Management Review,* October 1992, p. 18.
4. Ray Stata, "M.I.T. Conference on Transforming Organizations," May 30, 1990.
5. Jay A. Conger, *Learning to Lead,* San Francisco: Jossey-Bass, 1992.
6. Quoted in Conger, *op. cit.,* p. 49.
7. It should be noted that most vendors of leadership programs will create a dedicated, organization-specific program at a company's request. This approach allows companies to guide the content in a limited fashion. Such tailored programs are becoming more and more popular with companies.
8. "Why Executive Development Programs (Alone) Don't Work," in *Training & Development,* May 1992, p. 91.
9. For a very complete list of development activities, see Dave Ulrich and Dale Lake, *Organizational Capability,* New York: John Wiley & Sons, 1990, pp. 132–134.

Chapter 3. The "Thinking" Literacy Challenge

1. Robert W. Goddard, "Combating Illiteracy in the Workplace," *Management World,* March/April 1989, p. 8.
2. Anthony P. Carnevale, Leila J. Gainer, and Ann S. Meltzer, *Workplace Basics Training Manual,* San Francisco: Jossey-Bass Publishers, 1990, p. 1.
3. Reported in David Ulrich and Dale Lake, *Organizational Capability,* New York: John Wiley & Sons, 1990, pp. 4–5.
4. From a transcript of an oral history of training at Caterpillar, Inc., date unknown.

5. William Wiggenhorn, "Motorola U: When Training Becomes an Education," *Harvard Business Review,* July–August 1990, p. 77.
6. Story told by Charles J. Mitchell in "Real-World Basics," *Training,* February 1991, pp. 60–64.
7. Carnevale, Gainer, and Meltzer, *op. cit.,* p. 4.
8. Quotation from *Investing in People: The Key to Canada's Prosperity and Growth,* by Dr. Anil Verma and Deborah Irvine, Willowdale, Ontario: Information Technology Association of Canada, 1992, p. 19.
9. John Case, "A Company of Businesspeople," *Inc.,* April 1993, p. 86.
10. Quote in the *Newsletter* of the Business Council for Effective Literacy, July 1990, p. 7.
11. William Wiggenhorn, *op. cit.,* p. 78.
12. Story and quotation from the *Newsletter* of the Business Council for Effective Literacy, April 1992, p. 12.

Chapter 4. Overcoming Functional Myopia

1. Michael Hammer and James Champy, *Reengineering the Corporation,* New York: HarperBusiness, 1993, pp. 8–9.
2. Graham M. Palmer and Sherrill G. Burns, "Revolutionizing the Business: Strategies for Succeeding With Change," *Human Resources Quarterly,* February 1992, p. 79.
3. RAMS is a trademark of Digital Equipment Corporation.
4. Peter M. Senge, *The Fifth Discipline: The Art & Practice of the Learning Organization,* New York: Doubleday, 1990.
5. Alan F. White, "Organizational Transformation at BP: An Interview with Chairman and CEO Robert Horton," *Human Resource Planning,* vol. 15, no. 1, pp. 3–14.
6. Quoted in "Put Your Money Where Your Teams Are," by Rebecca Sisco, *Training,* July 1992, p. 42.
7. For an excellent discussion of how pay issues fit into a company's overall transformation initiatives, see *The High Performance Enterprise* by Donna R. Neusch and Alan F. Siebenaler, Essex Junction, VT: Oliver Wight Publications, 1993.
8. Quoted in "The Search for the Organization of Tomorrow," *Fortune,* May 18, 1992, p. 95.

Chapter 5. Building and Sustaining Effective "Learning" Teams

1. Clint Larson, "Team Tactics Can Cut Product Development Costs," in *The Journal of Business Strategy,* September/October 1988, pp. 22–25.
2. Quoted in "Multi-Skilled Teams Replace Old Work Systems," by D. Keith Denton, *HR Magazine,* September 1992, p. 49.
3. Quoted in John H. Zenger *et al., Leading Teams,* Homewood, IL: Business One Irwin, 1993, p. 226.
4. *Ibid.,* p. 249.
5. For an excellent treatment of networked teams, see Jessica Lipnack and Jeffrey Stamps, *The TeamNet Factor,* Essex Junction, VT: Oliver Wight Publications, Inc., 1993.
6. Quotation from "Human Integrated Manufacturing," *Chief Executive,* July/August 1992, p. 55.

Chapter 6. Managers as Enablers

1. Thomas R. Horton and Peter C. Reid, "What Fate for Middle Managers?," *Management Review,* January 1991, p. 22.
2. Quoted in "The Bureaucracy Busters," by Brian Dumaine, *Fortune,* June 17, 1991, p. 50.
3. Michael H. Morris and J. Don Trotter, "Institutionalizing Entrepreneurship in a Large Company: A Case Study at AT&T," *Industrial Marketing Management,* May 1990, pp. 131–139.
4. From "Making Over Middle Managers," by Kenneth Labich, *Fortune,* May 8, 1989, p. 64.
5. Laurence J. Peters, *The Peter Principle,* New York: William Morrow, 1969.

Chapter 7. Investing in People

1. *EDN,* March 19, 1992, p. 18.
2. Peter F. Drucker, *Post-Capitalist Society,* New York: HarperBusiness, 1993, p. 193.

3. "A Capital Idea," *Training,* January 1992, p. 32.
4. Quote in "Brainpower," by Thomas A. Stewart, *Fortune,* June 3, 1991, p. 54.
5. Robert B. Reich, *The Next American Frontier,* New York: Penguin Books, 1983, p. 236.
6. "Companies That Train Best," by Ronald Henkoff, *Fortune,* March 22, 1993, pp. 63–64.
7. William Davidow and Michael Malone, *The Virtual Corporation,* New York: HarperCollins, 1992, p. 185.

Chapter 8. Embracing New Ways of Learning

1. George Bernard Shaw, *Pygmalion,* New York: Penguin Books, 1951, p. 80.
2. "The Coming of the New Organization," *Harvard Business Review,* January–February 1988, p. 46.
3. It should be noted that a lot of progress has been made in defining industry standards and in the development of translation programs to make possible the sharing of information across diverse computing platforms. To date, the solutions tend to be costly and are often difficult to implement.
4. See Tichy and Sherman, *op. cit.,* p. 30.
5. *Ibid.*

Chapter 9. Breathing Life into the Learning Organization

1. Quotation from "Speed, Simplicity, Self-Confidence: An Interview with Jack Welch," by Noel Tichy and Ram Charan, *Harvard Business Review,* September–October 1989, p. 118.
2. "Times Are Good? Create a Crisis," by Brian Dumaine, *Fortune,* June 28, 1993, pp. 123–130.
3. *Ibid.,* p. 130.

Chapter 10. Creating a Virtual Training Organization

1. Information on Corning comes primarily from "Corning's Blueprint for Training in the '90s," by Sarah Lang, *Training,* July 1991, pp. 33–36.
2. *Ibid.,* p. 34.
3. *Ibid.,* p. 36.
4. Stephen S. McIntosh, Susan Page, and Kenneth B. Hall, "Adding Value Through Training," *Training & Development,* July 1993, p. 39.
5. *Ibid.*
6. *Ibid.,* p. 40.
7. Sarah Lang, *op. cit.,* p. 36.

Chapter 12. Nurturing Learning Beyond the Next Quarter

1. Noel M. Tichy and Stratford Sherman, *Control Your Destiny or Someone Else Will,* New York: Currency-Doubleday, 1993, p. 22.
2. David A. Garvin, "Building a Learning Organization," *Harvard Business Review,* July–August 1993, p. 85.
3. *Ibid.,* p. 86.
4. *Ibid.,* p. 87.

INDEX

ABOUT THE AUTHOR

Daniel R. Tobin is an independent consultant on corporate learning strategies. He has worked in the training and development field, in both industry and academia, for more than two decades. From 1981 to 1992, he was employed by Digital Equipment Corporation in a variety of training and development positions, most recently as Manufacturing Industries Executive Education Manager. Previous experience includes development manager for corporate management education, manager of sales and sales support training, and director of research and planning for a community college.

- Mr. Tobin has made presentations to such groups as:

- A workshop sponsored by the National Academy of Engineering.

- A U.S. Department of Defense Concurrent Engineering Symposium.

- A symposium on Managing Concurrent Engineering sponsored by the University of Southern California School of Business Administration.

Mr. Tobin holds a Master's degree from the Johnson Graduate School of Management and a Ph.D. in Economics of Education, both from Cornell University. He is a member of the American Society for Training and Development, the Society for Human Resource Management, and the National Speakers Association.